DRONE ADVISOR

Somesh Arora

&

Team Aviation

Sapphire & Sage Law Offices

Purchase of this book also provides 2 hours Free consulation from the Authors

and

further information on Drones for one year through emails..

Contact:- books@sapphireandsage.in

Acknowledgement

"I have to start by thanking my awesome team Akshita Agarwal, Juhi Rana, Arundhati Shrivastava and Ritika Garg (All recent law graduates of Jindal Global Law School). I address them Drone Girls who did fabulous job without which this book was a distant dream. Kudos my Co-Authors.

Special Thanks to Kay Wackwitz and Vivek Verma. They both were guiding brains in shaping this book. Thank you so much.

And a Big Thank to Shweta Rawat who was always on toes to take up any challenge to make this dream come true.

Foreword

- by Kay Wackwitz, CEO & Founder of Drone Industry Insights

We live in disruptive times where technology has an increasing influence on our life's. A lot of things became possible over the last few years that were pure science fiction a while back. Disruptive technologies came and allowed to do things very differently - more efficiently – and changed businesses and the way we live around the world.

In terms of drones, we are still at the beginning but with massive potential going forward. The drone industry market is valued at 42.8 billion USD in 2025. From generating 22.5 billion USD in 2020 it will grow at a CAGR[1] of 13.8% and nearly double in size over the course of the next five years.

This stable year on year growth is also a reflection of the ongoing high investments and the consolidation of the commercial drone market. The commercial drone industry continues to grow and remains resilient despite being strongly regulated. It has matured from hype and exponential growth to steady returns, increased adoption and is now heading towards stable and predictable growth.

Currently, the national drone markets in USA and China dominate the commercial drone market. Together their revenue makes up over two-thirds of the global drone market size and it is very unlikely to change in the foreseeable future. Asia in general will continue to build onto this growth and become the leading region by a considerable margin.

The main reasons for this are the huge population and the value drones can create for them. Furthermore, when it comes to connecting rural areas with bigger cities, drones can leapfrog the costly step of creating new ground infrastructure. Urgent deliveries, such as blood donations or Covid19 tests can be transferred to very remote locations in a very short time.

This booklet shall provide you with an overview of the current technology, methods and industries in which drones are being used. To bring all this potential in the sky, a thorough understanding of the regulatory environment is essential.

Let's strive for nothing less than using this disruptive potential and use drones to make our planet a better, healthier and more sustainable place.

Yours sincerely,

- Kay Wackwitz

About Kay Wackwitz

Kay Wackwitz is the CEO & Founder of Drone Industry Insights, the leading European market research company for commercial drones. He has a degree in aeronautical engineering and more than 18 years of experience in manned and unmanned aviation, from which he's developed in-depth knowledge and an extensive network. His expertise is shared via numerous international consulting assignments, and he is recognized globally as an expert in commercial drone applications of all industrial verticals.

Contents

I. CHAPTER 1

INTRODUCTION

A. What is a drone?

A drone, also known as an Unmanned Aircraft (UA), or an Unmanned Aerial Vehicle (UAV), is a type of aircraft, which is operated without any pilot on board of the aircraft. A drone can be either controlled by a pilot on the ground through a remote or, can fly autonomously through pre-installed software in their systems.

i. Classification of drones:

Given below is a table with pictorial representation of various classifications of drones used in the industry in India.

Picture	Category
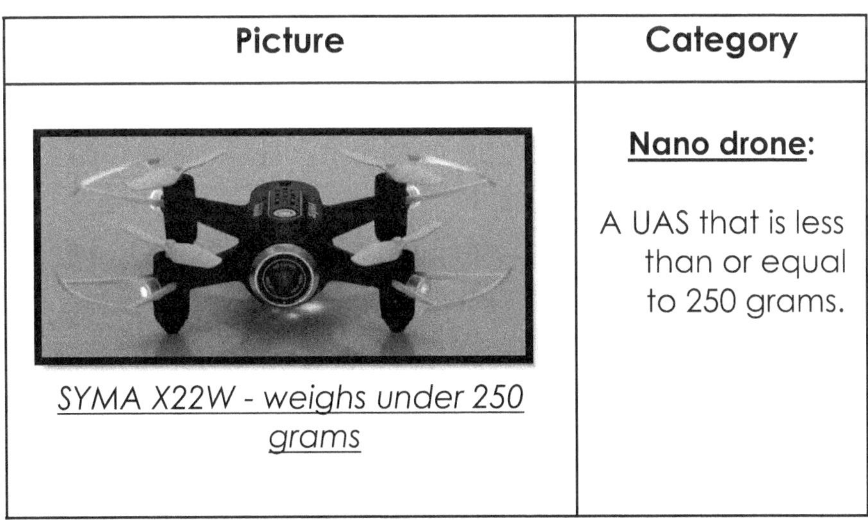 *SYMA X22W - weighs under 250 grams*	**Nano drone:** A UAS that is less than or equal to 250 grams.

 **NINJA UAV – weighs up to 2 kilograms**	**Micro Drone:** A UAS Greater than 250 gram and less than or equal to 2 kilograms.
 *DJI Matrice 200 - weighs approx. 3.80 kilograms*	**Small Drone:** A UAS Greater than 2 kilograms and less than or equal to 25 kilograms
 *Vulcan UAV Air lift weighs approx. 30 kgs.*	**Medium Drone:** A UAS Greater than 25 kilograms and less than or equal to 150 kilograms.

DRDO Rustom- 1 – weighs 800 kilograms

Large Drone:

A UAS Greater than 150 kilograms.

ii. Types of Drones:

Below are various types of drones used in the Drone Industry:-

Picture	Type
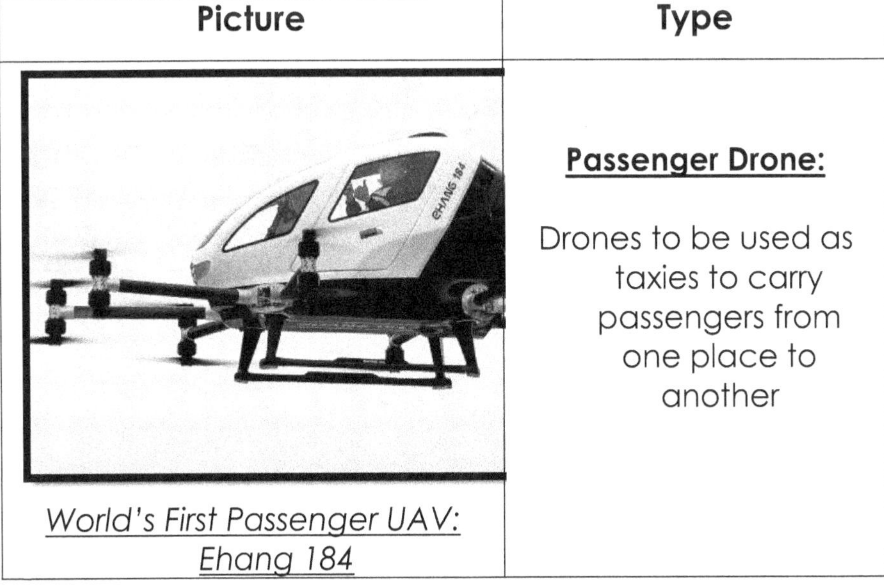 *World's First Passenger UAV: Ehang 184*	**Passenger Drone:** Drones to be used as taxies to carry passengers from one place to another

Multi-Rotor Drone:

One of the cheapest drone options available in the market. Further classifies into Tricopter (3 rotor), Quadcopter (4 rotor), Hexacopter(6 rotor), & Octocopter (8 rotor)

Single Rotor Helicopter Drone:

These drones look similar to an actual Helicopter. Single rotor drones are more efficient than a multi-rotor drone. They have more stability and higher-flying time.

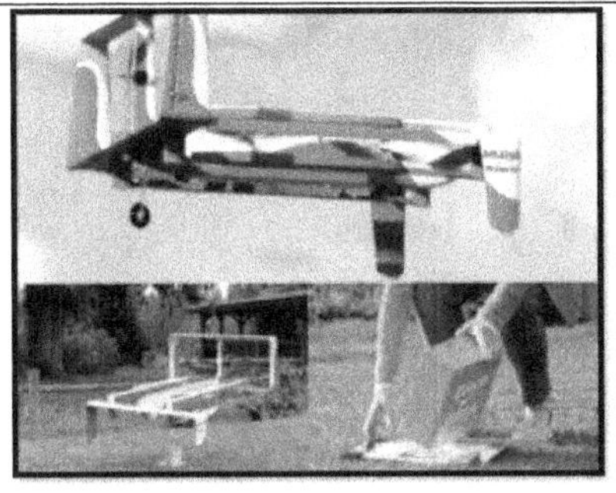

<u>Fixed Wing Drone with a tail rotor:</u>

Used by amazon for contactless delivery

B. <u>Sub - components of a Drone</u>

Drones have the following sub - components:

1. Standard Propellers – they are the tractor propeller usually in front of the drones. They pull the drones through the air. They could be made out of plastic as well as carbon fibre. R&D is still going on to make the propellers more efficient. Propellers are responsible for the direction and motion of the drone. Maintenance of all propellers is thus extremely important.
2. Pusher Propellers – these propellers are responsible for forward and backward thrust. Generally located at the back of the drone. Even pusher propellers can be made out of plastic or carbon fibre. R&D is being carried out to make these propellers also more efficient for the flight.
3. Brushless Motors – an addition to motors to make them more efficient and save battery life. This also softens the noises made by the drones while flying.
4. Landing Gear – landing gear depends on how big the drone is and for what purpose it is being used. It is not necessary to have landing gear in

small drones, but larger drones which cover longer distances generally have fixed landing gear. Drones with cameras can face a problem with the landing gear restricting the view. However, the gear makes the drone safer.

5. Electronic Speed Controllers (ESC) – a device to check the speed and direction of the drone along with variations of brakes. This also converts DC battery power to AC power to propel the brushless motors. It is located in the mainframe of the drone.

6. Flight controller – the motherboard of the drone. Processes messages from the pilot to the drone. It interprets input from the receiver, the GPS Module, the battery monitor and the onboard sensors. Responsible for the speed, directions and inputs from ESC. All commands such as autopilot, switching on the camera, autonomous functions are controlled by the flight controller.

7. The receiver – responsible for the radio signals sent from the controller to the drone. A minimum number of channels needed are generally 4, the recommendation is however for 5.

8. The transmitter – transmits radio signals from the controller to the drone for flight commands and directions. Like the 'receiver' needs 4 channels but 5 are recommended. Receiver and transmitter can have one radio signal for communication. Radio signals help distinguish one drone from another via a standard code.

9. GPS Module – responsible for the longitude, latitude and elevation points of the drone. Helps navigate longer distances and capture details of specific locations on land. This is the device which helps the drone in safely returning

home/controller even in case connection or signal is lost.

10. Battery – the powerhouse of the drone. Size of the drone determines the size of the battery needed, smaller the drone, smaller the battery and vice versa. Battery monitor on the drone helps the controller keep a check on the battery level and the overall performance of the battery.

11. Camera – drones come with both inbuilt as well as detachable cameras. Helps in taking photos, videos which form an important function for the drone users. Types and quality of the camera vary in the market.

12. Gimbal – a pivoting mount for the stabilization of cameras.

13. Sensors – used for filming, mapping etc. Several types of sensors like thermal, LiDAR etc. Sensors are used for 3D photogrammetry images, 3D mapping. The sensors can be used with software to process the data. Many companies which do mapping use this technology for the same.

14. Collision Avoidance Sensors – as the name suggests, these sensors protect the drone from a collision. In the process they use, monocular vision, ultrasonic (sonar), infrared, LiDAR, time of flight and vision sensors.

These form the basic components of a drone, without parts 1 to 11 a drone would not function. Additions can be made further but the above-mentioned parts are necessary. The following pictures will help in recognizing the components of a drone on a physical model:

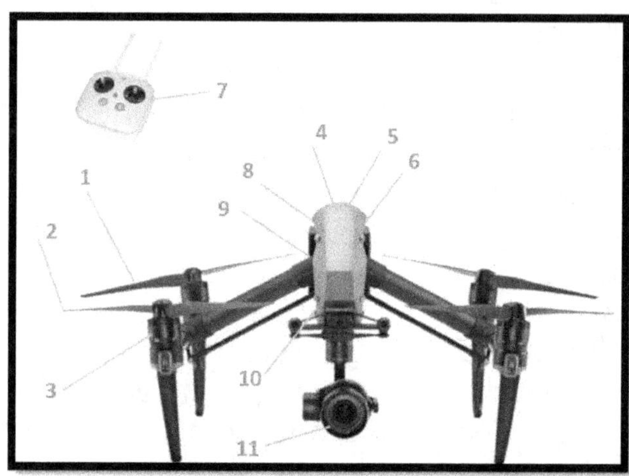

7
4
5
6
1
8
9
2
3
10
11

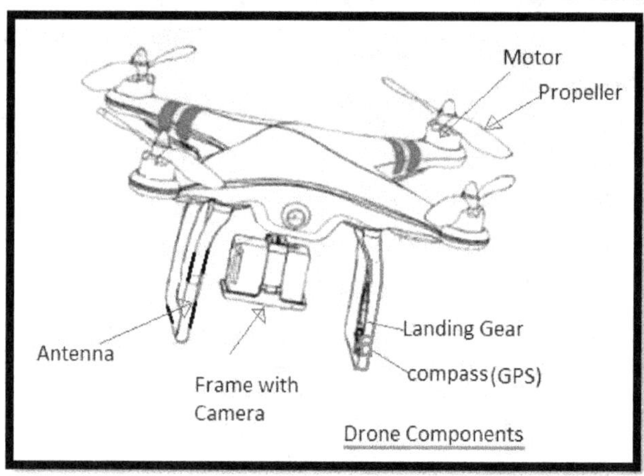

Motor
Propeller
Antenna
Landing Gear
compass(GPS)
Frame with
Camera
Drone Components

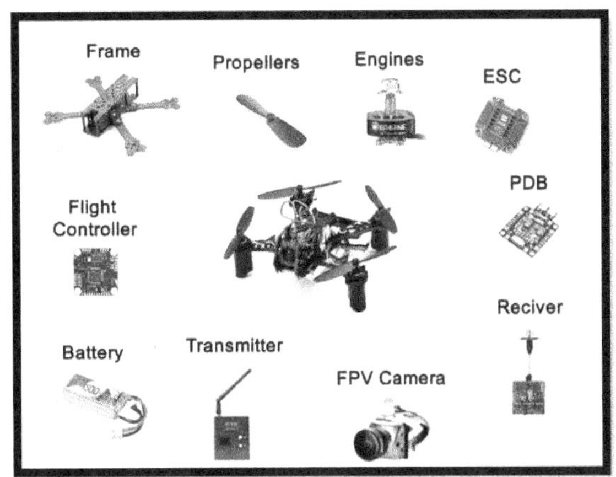
Frame
Propellers
Engines
ESC
PDB
Flight
Controller
Reciver
Battery
Transmitter
FPV Camera

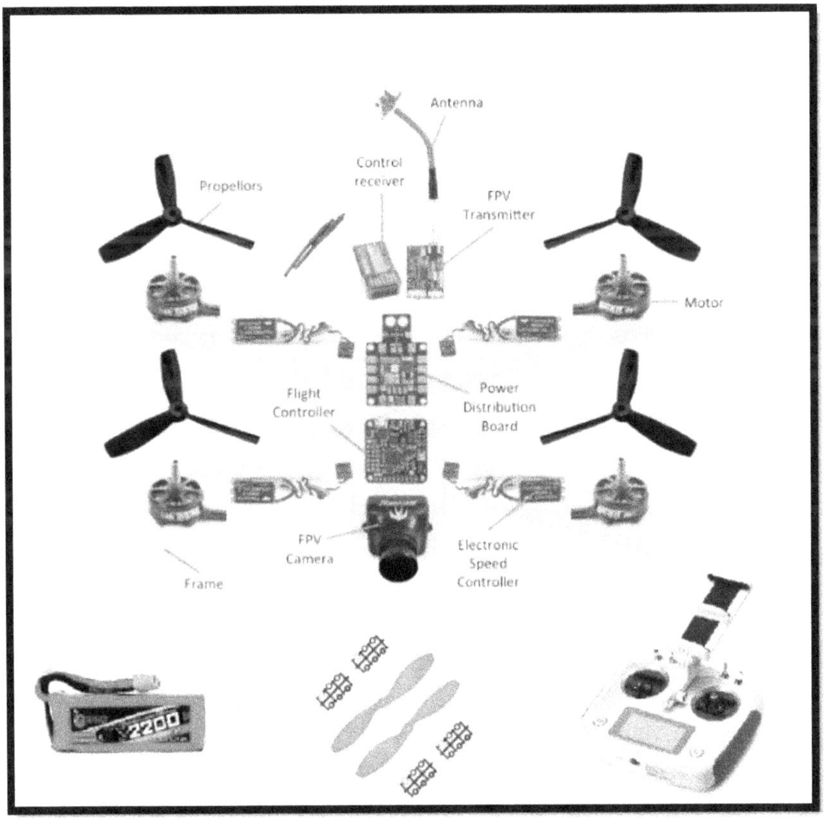

Antenna
Control
receiver
FPV
Transmitter
Propellors
Motor
Flight
Controller
Power
Distribution
Board
FPV
Camera
Electronic
Speed
Controller
Frame
2200

II. CHAPTER 2

USAGE OF DRONES

A. Surveillance and law enforcement

Drones are being used for surveillance across the world to make sure that the citizens follow the rules that are made for them. Different government departments use drones for different kinds of surveillance. Following are the usages:

Uses of drones:

- The police department uses drones for analyzing and searching for illegal activities.
- Remote area inspection
- Traffic surveillance and management
- Risk assessment
- Event security
- Perimeter control
- Tactical surveillance
- Prison surveillance
- Monitoring of big crowds at gatherings and protests

B. Security and Defence

The primary usage of drones by government entities in India is in the field of security and defence. With the development of high camera resolution, artificial intelligence and various other features, drones are becoming a very attractive option for the Armed Forces of India.

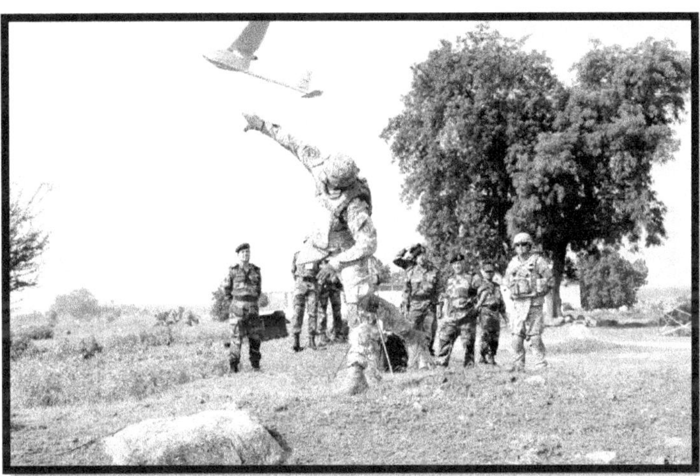

Uses of Drone

- Monitoring/Surveillance/ Reconnaissance- UAVs are used for gathering aerial intelligence and information gathering.
- Identification and tracking of insurgents, vehicles, weapons, explosive devices
- Delivering of Medical Aids and Supplies

C. <u>Disaster Management</u>

Rapid climate changes in the world, which are triggering natural disasters, require the government authorities to upgrade their existing disaster management strategies and systems by using advanced technologies. Drones are one such technology in the market that can serve the purpose of emergency response, which are also capable of rescue operations. Their role is not just limited to real-time surveillance and search & rescue, but can also help in the delivery of essential medical supplies and food items to affected areas.

<u>Usage of Drones:</u>

- The National Disaster Management Authority (NDMA), deployed around 4 drones during the flood in Uttarakhand to scan the areas which the search & rescue teams could not physically access. They carried out reconnaissance activities of 50 locations to assess the damage. Drones were able to spot around 190 dislocated people in forests, hills and other isolated areas.

Additionally, their State Management Authority has also procured a fleet of 10 drones for rescue operations.
- In Mandi, Himachal Pradesh, when 24 engineering students were swept away by the Beas River, drones were utilized by the National Disaster Relief Force (NDRF) to track their location.
- During the 2014 Malin landslide in Ambegaon taluka, the NDRF deployed drones at the site of the disaster, where they covered an area of 2.5 kms, and live-streamed the visuals to the control room.
- In 2017, a terror attack on pilgrims on their way to Amarnath Yatra took
  place. The Central Reserve Police Force (CRPF), who were responsible for the safety of the pilgrims, used camera drones to keep a watch over the tourist traffic on the Amarnath Yatra route. The famous drone 'Netra' was also deployed to keep surveillance on the pilgrimage.
- Moreover, drones are capable of transmitting a live video feed in high resolution of disaster-struck areas which can help in creating 3D models for effective decision making
- It can be used as a container to carry essential goods where humans can't reach and provide medical aid, food and water supplies.

D. Agriculture

The use of Unmanned Aerial System (UAS) in Agriculture enables agricultural practices to be performed in a sustainable manner using Optimal technology.

Usage of Drone

- The Application of Drones in Agriculture ranges from Soil & Field Analysis, Planting Crops and Trees, Crop Spraying, Irrigation Scheduling, Crop Monitoring, Weed Identification, Crop Health Assessment, Crop Insurance, Geo-Fencing and Livestock management.
- The UAS provides real-time data in greater aspect with less error as compared to the satellite data.

E. Agritech

35 startups in India have started work on AgriTech. It is a project which is not very affordable. For farmers most of the time, even if they are able to buy a drone, maintenance becomes difficult and expensive. Analyzing data and studying the outcome also requires software, AI and man force. Agritech is a growing industry which focuses on the improvement of the

agricultural sector with the help of technology and scientific analysis.

Usage of drones:

- Calculate land sizes
- Classify types of crops
- Perform soil mapping
- Pest management
- Plan their harvest
- Mapping to improve irrigation systems and agricultural yields
- Crop rotation
- Aquaponics and hydroponics
- Fish farming
- Biowaste management
- Organic farming
- Bio-based crop protection
- Predict crop yield
- Analyse plant health

- Remote sensing data – timely action to prevent crop loss from diseases, optimize irrigation, reduce the impact of climate change and unpredictable seasonal variations.

F. <u>Mining</u>

Drones can provide valuable data for mining sites. This data can be used to ensure the safety of the workers on site. It can provide precise measurements of the area, and it saves up the cost.

<u>Usage of Drones</u>

- Inspection & Monitoring - it is an easy and efficient way to closely monitor and control the operations at the mining site. As it is a dangerous industry for workers, inspection can help in determining the work conditions.
- Surveying & Mapping- it can provide valuable data with precise measurements which can assist

in mining operations. The data will also help in maintaining safety and enhancing security.

- Stockpile management- it can provide aerial view of the inventory so the proper records can be maintained of stockpile movement.
- Haulage road optimization- aerial data can be collected to provide for safe transit, road conditions can be monitored to plan and maintain the facility.
- Tailing dam management –mining operations produce waste product stockpiles during mineral separations, so drones can be used in overlooking the maintenance of trailing dams to prevent any mishap.
- Exploring minerals- drones can be used to explore minerals where it is difficult to navigate physically by foot. It also saves up on time.

G. Conservation and Wildlife

UAVs can be used for monitoring species of different groups of living organisms like animals, plants or other living organisms and also used in mapping their ecology, their natural environment in which a particular species of organism lives.

Usage of drones;

- Used in monitoring a wide range of species like birds, reptiles, marine species such as turtles, whales, dolphins and dugongs.
- Used in studies of species in abundance, in places where humans cannot easily and safely reach or where the functions cannot be performed as efficiently and in due time. Drones can provide insights into the wildlife ecology and vegetation mechanism.
- Remote use of drones provides non-hazardous, less invasive, reliable monitoring technique to collect data and document the wildlife health and habitat.
- Sensors can be attached to drones to collect acoustic sound recording of birds.
- Tracking systems can be attached to drones to collect wildlife movement and environment data.
- Used in detecting any danger or damage that might occur in a protected area through mapping.

- Used in Epidemiological and Zoonotic Studies (the branches of medicine which deal with the incidence, distribution, and control of diseases).
- Used to protect elephants, rhinos, lions, leopards etc. from the attention of poachers and wildlife traffickers by monitoring poacher movements.
- Used to benefit in responsible tourism and eco-education through videos of remote animal population.

H. Emergency Response and Rescue

A UAS can access difficult terrains and fly at minimum altitudes that even an aircraft cannot. Thus making the best alternative for Emergency Response and Rescue.

Uses of Drones

- Emergency Rescue: They enable faster search and rescue operations. The UAS in rescue operations reduces manpower, requires lesser resources and even time is significantly reduced.
- The UAS can examine the ground from above with a high definition video technology and thermal imaging to locate victims and fleeing criminals.
- Emergency Response: UAS provides the optimal solution to respond under emergency situations. These include missing persons, fire situations, possible suicide, crowd safety, bomb-threats, animal rescue, chemical spillages and light aircraft crashes.

- The UAS can easily respond in such circumstances, as there is no obstacle or danger to it and can aid the emergency response team as well.

I. <u>Healthcare</u>

Drones are helping in the delivery of various medical supplies like vaccine, medications to places where they are required and to rural areas where proper infrastructure for medical treatment is not available. Drones can provide mobile healthcare facilities to patients more rapidly and efficiently. Patients can be cared and nursed from home than going to the hospital with the use of a drone.

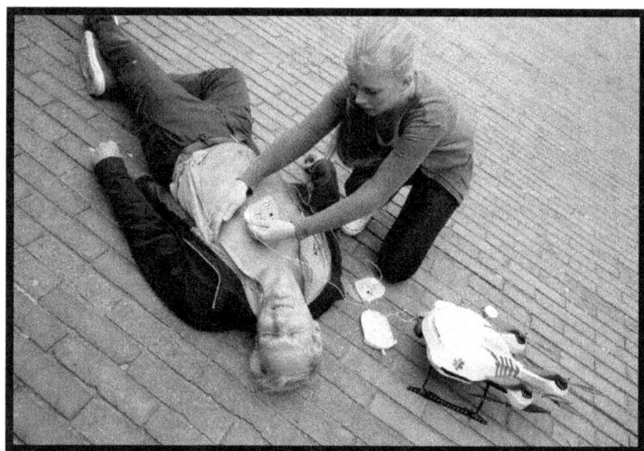

<u>Uses of Drone:</u>

- Transporting blood sample: from a small and remote area to the laboratories for testing.
- Delivery of first aid kits and medications: in time of emergency.

- Perform CPR: with the use of ambulance drones designed specifically to perform CPR until the emergency services arrive and handle the case.
- Delivering medicines, vaccines, equipment: that is relevant in emergency situations.
- In Indian Scenario: National disaster management authority (NDMA) has used drones in disaster relief and rescue in India. A drone was used to transport a single unit of blood from a remote healthcare centre in Uttarakhand's Tehri district and many such government initiatives are coming up to use drones in providing healthcare services.

J. <u>Disease Control</u>

As the pandemic of 2020 unfolded, the world realized the need for a technology to track diseases in order to control them. Major outbreaks of diseases leading to epidemics or pandemics have been due to zoonotic diseases. Drones make it easier for scientists to track animals from spreading such diseases.

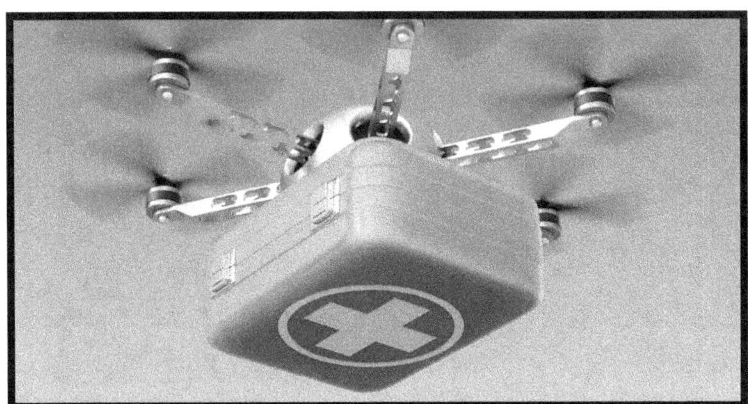

<u>Usage of drones:</u>

- Tracking animals
- With the help of thermal cameras tracking malaria in red zones have become easier
- Study of animal movements help explain the jump of viruses from animals to humans
- Catch various kinds of animals and insects to inspect potentially dangerous viruses within them
- Tracking agricultural grounds for worms spreading diseases through food.

K. <u>Urban Planning</u>

With the advancement of technology for drones, it has become easier for institutions, governments to survey and have accurate data of any city. It helps in the development and the growth of a city in a more organized manner. Two kinds of technology that can be used for urban mapping are LiDAR or Photogrammetry.

<u>Uses of drones:</u>

- Land surveying/ cartography – helps in measuring the distances as well as the variations in heights on the land.
- Land management and development – making a city precise city plan is easier with the usage of drones and thus it helps in the management and development of old and new zones.
- Precise measurements – volumetric, surface, etc.
- Slope monitoring – it is easier to measure various degrees of slopes across the city for underground as well as on the surface planning.
- Urban planning

L. <u>Construction</u>

Industries like construction rely on continuous innovation to grow, one such development has been that of drones in the industry.

<u>Uses of drones:</u>

- Mapping of construction locations
- Modelling of constructions projects

- Development in the pre-construction period
- Keeping a check on the quality of work
- Detection of trespassers or unauthorized people
- Improving safety
- Real-time data analysis
- Real-time 3D models
- Efficient inventory management
- Mitigating risks
- Tracking progress difficult or inaccessible areas after construction
- Maintenance of inspection data
- Detecting defects
- Post-disaster check-ups
- Binford Robotics are using their drones for Construction Automation
- Architectural Designing and planning

M. Inventory/ Warehouse Management

Drones can help in the management of the inventory, so humans don't need to do such tiresome and dangerous tasks. With the advancement in drones, they now come with navigation systems and sensors, it will help in making the job of management quick and easy.

Uses of Drones:

- Inspection and Surveillance- it can replace the manual inspection. High Racks, shelf, etc. and other dangerous areas of inventory can be easily inspected without the use of ladders.
- Inventory management- counting, item search, maintenance, audits can be comfortably done with the use of a drone. Drones add value to improve the process.
- Intra-Logistics- Movement of the item from one place to another can be done with the help of delivery drones.

N. Waste Management

The UAS has made it easier to contain waste management in many ways.

Uses of Drones:

- Landfill Monitoring – Drones can capture high-resolution images and create 3D models to help in monitoring landfills.
- Airspace Calculation – Drones can help waste management organizations in measuring overfill capacity and remaining airspace of a landfill.
- Landfill Cell Management - Drones can help waste management organization and in achieving the best compaction rate.
- Garbage Collection - Drones can identify litterbugs and collect littered garbage at public places like parks and benches.
- Power-Lines Cleaning - Power Companies can employ drones to clean the power lines using the flame throwers. The UAS can burn garbage such as Plastic bags, lanterns and litter that are stuck on the power lines.

O. <u>Rural Development</u>

The Survey of India, Department of Revenue, Panchayati Department of State Government, Union Panchayati Raj Ministry are all involved in the project Swamitva Yojana.

This project has also teamed the Survey of India (SOI), National Mapping Agency (NMA), under the Ministry of Science and Technology to employ professional grade drones for Large Scale Mapping (LSM).

<u>Uses of Drone:</u>

- The Survey Of India (SOI) plans to deploy drones that will map in high resolution of 1:500 scale covering all the village areas with the help of the GIS Database.
- The 3D Maps that will be created will see the two necessary steps. Firstly, the preparation of Orthorectified image base map at 1:500 scale with an accuracy of + 10 cm. Followed by GIS Data Preparation as per the requirement of each state.
- The State of Karnataka has also been working on developing Geo-Referenced Land-Based Records.
- The Drone Technology will cover the unmapped territories like canals, canal limits, village boundaries, agricultural field limits and roads in villages.
- The UAS will implement in formulating records-land records, socio-economic data that is beneficial to both the Government and the Common Man. For the Govt, the records will aid in

better decision making and for the common man, they will have an actual property and legal title to their lands.

- The goal for SOI is to successfully map 660,000 villages by 2024 via the UAS. Before the end of this fiscal year, SOI will have managed to survey 100,000 villages in India.

P. Energy

Drones are helping in the smooth functioning of the Energy Sector. They are playing an important role in monitoring and inspecting the solar, wind, oil and gas energy industry and helping in adhering to the safety standards effectively.

Drones are useful for this sector as they can inspect in areas that are hard to reach, it eliminates the safety risks that are there in physical inspection, it reduced the inspection time and it is cost-efficient.

Uses of drones:

- Used in the inspection of wind energy. Drones can provide information through 2D and 3D images of any damage that might be on the turbine for an easy and quick inspection.

- Used in survey and inspection solar panels. The drones can provide images and videos of the solar panels which can be used in efficient maintenance of the solar panel of regular basis.
- Used in the inspection of Oil and Gas industry. It also helps in detecting any damage or violation of any safety standards through monitoring and therefore adhering to regulations.
- Used in the inspection of power lines. Drones being speedy and involving less risk can be used in the surveys of the power lines, to inspect lines that might have been damaged due to bad weather or
- any other possible reason. Images can be obtained through drones and quick response can be taken in case of any fault in the power lines.

Q. Research purposes

Drones can provide highly accurate data, it can reach places with harsh environments and conditions, it has a high payload capacity, it is easy to operate and therefore it is recommended for use in research.

<u>Uses of Drones:</u>

Drones are used in aerial data collection for the research projects. Here are some examples of the research area where drones can be used.

- Agriculture research
- Archaeological research
- Arctic research
- Capturing the spread of algae
- Climate observation
- Counting animal populations
- Environmental monitoring
- Ethnographic research
- Examining coastal regions
- Flying over historical buildings and sites
- Forestry and Natural Resources Management
- Geophysical surveying
- Glacier surveillance
- Iceberg monitoring

- Identification of plant species
- Mapping coastal regions
- Mapping of excavation sites
- Mapping sandbars – measuring
- Mapping the movement of sandbars
- Measuring nuclear contamination
- Meteorological research
- Ocean & sea research support
- Photogrammetry
- Radiation measurement
- Radiation monitoring
- Recording salt water infiltration
- Sensor research for RPA
- Studying biodiversity
- Surveillance of sea mammals
- Volcanic eruptions

R. <u>Maritime</u>

Drones can help in the operation of various maritime uses. It is cost-effective and does the job quickly.

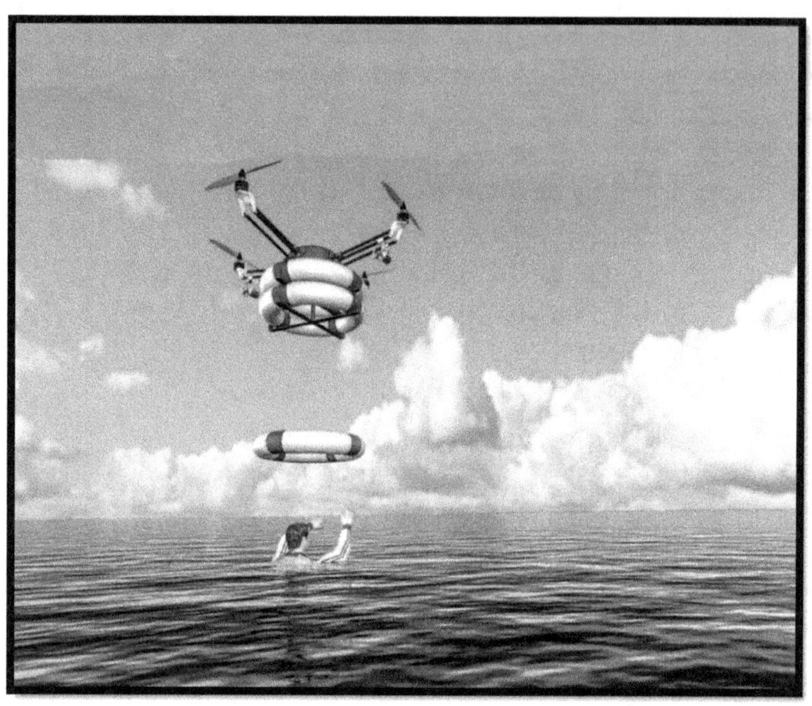

<u>Uses of Drones:</u>

- Inspection- data can be collected in a faster, cheaper and safer way with the use of drones. It replaces the need for human inspection
- Maintenance and repair- it can be monitored through drone surveys making it safe and efficient process.
- Security and Surveillance- used in border patrol, detection of any illegal activities and other maritime security-related operations.
- Search and Rescue- drones can be used in finding and rescue people.
- Ship Deliveries- used in transferring supplies, spare part and other material to the ship.
- Pollution detection and oil spill monitoring

- Construction- used to overlook the construction at ports

S. Tourism & Hospitality

The UAS is a great marketing tool to advertise luxury hotels, resorts, destinations, attractions and tours.

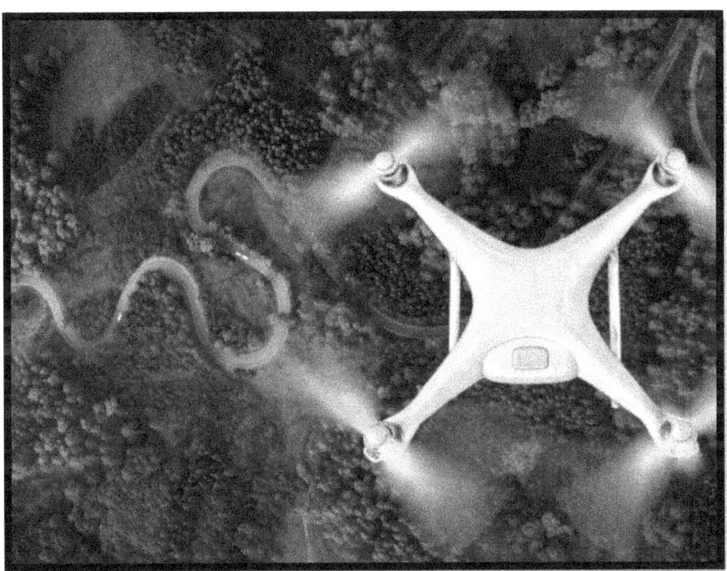

Uses of Drone:

- Leading Hotels and Resorts such as Waldorf Astoria and Conrad are replacing their traditional photo galleries on their websites with the UAS Video Footage.
- "Drones over Dolphine Strangers and Whales of Dana Point and Mani" was the first video that used drone videos for Wildlife Tourism.

T. <u>Professional Photography for events</u>

With the help of high-quality cameras, it is now possible to capture great views from drones. It is not an expensive device when compared to the price of normally available good quality camera and lenses, plus it is easy to fly a drone. Drones can photograph hard to reach areas, it allows you to shoot from height, provides possibility of creativity and innovation and it is fun to use as a hobby.

<u>Uses of Drones:</u>

- Real Estate Photography- used in capturing the aerial view of property and will be beneficial in Real Estate.
- Sports Photography- used in capturing photographs of sports player while on the field. Rather than having multiple cameras on different location to capture the movement of sports player, drones can be used during sports events.

- Filmmaking- earlier the cinematographer used to take aerial shots by hiring a helicopter which a costly method, with the help of drones now they can easily shoot at relatively low cost.
- Wedding or Party Photography- used to capture the wedding or any party event with the drones.

U. Professional video recording for the entertainment industry

Entertainment industry has shifted from using expensive methods like helicopters to more inexpensive like drones for their aerial shots. Industry has evolved by using drones for a more advanced videos of action scenes to showcasing destinations around the world and much more.

Uses of drones:

- Aerial documentary
- Aerial photography
- Cinematography
- Sports
- Light shows
- Advertisements

V. Delivery

The Ministry of Civil Aviation (MoCA), has already taken a big step towards conducting experiments for BVLOS operations in India, by inviting applications from the industrial players in the drone industry. Various delivery companies like Zomato, Swiggy and Dunzo have formed consortiums with other industries to share their expertise with them and building an effective drone delivery mechanism. Various companies like Amazon, Walmart, UPS etc. globally are investing in drone delivery projects and it can soon become a reality in the commercial sector.

Uses of drones:

Drones can be used to deliver various things like:-

- Food items for contactless delivery
- Medical supplies like medicines, vaccines, blood samples, food & water etc. to disaster-affected out of reach areas.
- Delivery of packages and/or mail.

W. <u>Drone Taxi</u>

Even though drones are in a developmental stage, innovations and research are always being carried out to enhance the experience and to grow the industry.

<u>Uses of drone:</u>

- Transportation
- Passenger travel
- Goods delivery
- Manned stunt drone

X. <u>Sports Broadcasting</u>

The sports industry aims to bring the viewers closer to action by incorporating new technology for live streaming to improve the fan experience. Using drones by the broadcasters will provide the industry with innovative ways to capture sporting events. Drones provide flexibility to the broadcasters by allowing them to use this lightweight technology with fitted cameras, and deliver high quality and real-time images and videos at various angles and let them get closer shots, which an individual fixed camera can't provide.

Uses of Drones:

- An Indian Startup Quidich, has helped in live aerial videography of IPL matches. It caters to BCCI, ICC and Star Sports.
- In the X games held in 2015, drones were used by broadcaster ESPN.
- Fox Sports used them for the coverage of golf's U.S Open.
- Sports channels like Fox Sports, ESPN, and Sky Sports are extensively using drones for covering every sports broadcast on their channel
- Drones can also help a coach who can use them to analyze his team's next opponent.
- They are also used in collecting data and recording statistics in sports

leagues that are played throughout the year.
- Drone Racing League

Y. <u>Outer Space</u>

Drone Technology has already conquered Earth and now they're heading out into the solar system. Nasa announced that it will launch two rotorcraft into the outer space in the next seven years.

<u>Uses of drones:</u>

- The NASA's Kennedy Space Centre is responsible for developing UAS that can explore other planets and asteroids.
- UAS is the best aid for an astronaut if in duration of the space mission there is any problem that arises.
- The main function of a UAS is to act as an alternative for NASA's Rovers.

- NASA has invested in Extreme Access Drones that are capable of withstanding inhospitable conditions of space and carry out 'hunt and gather' task from inaccessible places.

Z. <u>Telecommunication</u>

The sector can benefit from drones by way of maintenance, repairs, tower and wire check-ups, etc.

<u>Uses of drones:</u>

- Tower inspections
- Wire inspections
- Data collection from towers
- Tower maintenance
- Radio planning (signals)
- Detection of clear paths between antennas

- Land mapping for a clear plan
- Post-disaster management
- 4G LTE and 5G enabled drones for remote and post-disaster areas

AA.   Advertising

Just like filming has become easy for the entertainment industry, even shooting advertisements have taken advantage of the growing drones industry.

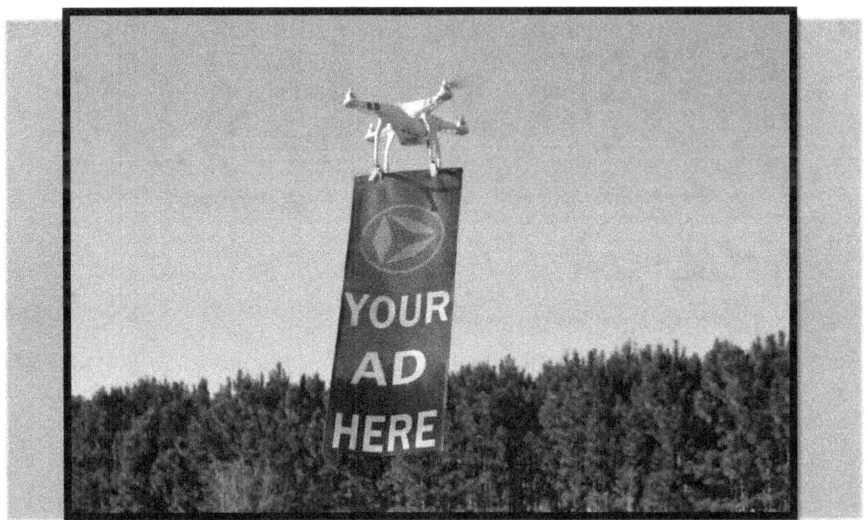

Uses of drones:

- Physical mediums for marketing
- Aerial advertisements
- Shooting of luxury cars
- Advertisements for Travel destinations
- Advertisement for sports competitions, leagues

BB.   Recreational/ outdoor uses

Around the world, private members of the society have been using drones for recreational activity. With less restrictions, it is easier for individuals to earn from photography or videos being shot from drones.

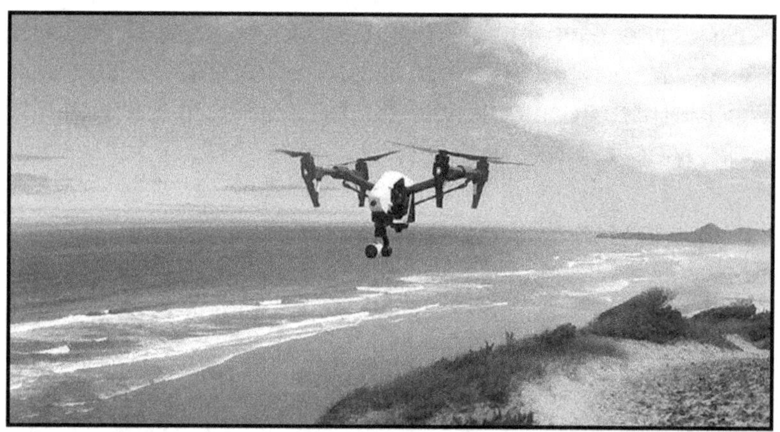

Uses of drone:

- Vacation/ tourist destinations
- Photography of difficult to reach areas
- Videos of the land and the ocean from an overshot point of view
- Aerial shots of sporting events
- Travel vlogs
- Mountain mapping for ease of climbers and skiers

CC.   Navigation System

Navigation UAS or GPS UAS provides the pilot/controller with necessary visual data that otherwise would not be known.

Uses of Drone:

- The UAS has the following navigational features: Position Hold, Return to home navigation, autonomous flight mode.
- Navigation occurs in two ways: <u>GNSS</u>- Global Navigation Satellite System (GNSS). In this UAS works with the Satellite Imagery, to procure data and collect images of any given territory. <u>Inertial Navigation</u> - The UAS uses its Inertial Measurement Unit (IMU) Sensor to navigate its way through. It's bound to use the IMU sensor as there is blockage either by man-made and natural structures and buildings that obstruct the satellite signals. The IMU sensor, however, has many faults to its own, as many of the times the sensor gives error in data and thus makes it crash.

DD. <u>COVID 19 outbreak</u>

During the 2020 global pandemic due to COVID 19 outbreak, drones were put to the test around the world. With the flexibility of no human connection involved, drones have helped nations to provide help, medicines, documents etc. to remote places and even to sanitize streets, buildings etc. around the country.

<u>Uses during the outbreak:</u>

- Surveillance: being used by law enforcement authorities such as the local police, municipal authorities etc. to keep a check on citizens who aren't following the rules, to break up social gatherings.
- Broadcast: being used to broadcast messages, information about lockdown measures, as well as warning citizens who are not following the rules.
- Disinfectant spraying: spraying disinfectant in potentially affected areas.
- Medicine and grocery deliveries: medical and testing samples are been delivered from hospitals to testing laboratories, pharmacies across the world. It is the safest and the quickest method while keeping the workers safe.
- Israel built a network of urban delivery drones for medicines and test samples to hospitals, pharmacies and laboratories.

I. CHAPTER 3

ESSENTIALS FOR DRONE COMPANIES

A. Incorporation

I. **Deciding the structure of business**
A start-up firstly has to decide whether they want to be incorporated as a Private Limited Company or a Limited Liability Partnership.

A Private Limited Company is a voluntary association of not less than two and not more than fifty members for a commercial purpose. Under this structure of business, the liability of its members is limited to the extent of their shareholding. And the transfer of its shares is limited to its members as they are restricted from allowing the public from subscribing to their shares and debentures.

A limited Liability Partnership (LLP) is like any partnership arrangement. There is no joint liability and therefore, no partner is made liable on account of the independent and unauthorized actions of other partners. LLP is therefore, a body corporate that exists separate from its members. The minimum number of members can be two and there is no cap on the maximum number of members.

The major differences between the two include,

1. In terms of **recognition**, since the Private Limited Company business has been in existence for a longer period, it enjoys more recognition in the country and therefore, has better established

procedures in places. LLPs are still developing in terms of regulation.

2. In terms of **funding**, it is easier for Companies to raise funding because partnerships cannot issue shares and thereby, are unable to attract equity funding effectively expand their business.

3. For **registration requirements**, both Pvt. Ltd. Co. and an LLP have to follow certain regulatory compliances such as obtaining a Digital Signatures Certificate (DSC) and obtaining a Director Identification Number (DIN) for directors. Both requires name approval from MCA and must file for incorporation. However, Pvt. Ltd Co. has to file MOA and AOA with he Registrar of Companies whereas the LLP has to file a LLP agreement.

4. In terms of **cost**, setting up an LLP is relatively cheaper. It requires around 15,000/- for registration and 4000/- for compliance with MCA regulations. A Company needs around 20,000/- to start and another 15,000/- for annual maintenance of the company.

5. A Pvt. Ltd co. is more organized in terms of **structure**. There is a clear demarcation between the owners and the management which is not present in an LLP. In a Company, the Shareholders do not participate in the management of the business.

6. In terms of **Compliance requirements**, an LLP has lesser compliance procedures as compared to a Limited Company. For instance, they do not have to audit its books of accounts if their revenue is less than 40 lakhs or capital contribution is less than 25 lakhs. In terms of violation of these

requirements, a Pvt. Ltd Co. would have to pay higher fines.

7. The **tax benefits** for LLPs are also higher since they just have to file two forms, income tax and alternative minimum tax whereas the Company has to pay a tax of the earning of the company, dividend distribution tax and alternate minimum tax.

Therefore, we can see that in terms of setting up a business, an LLP is a more attractive option however from the point of view of an investor, a Private Limited Company is a more attractive option.

II.   **Process for Incorporation**

- To begin incorporation, the start-ups can approach the traditional method of setting up a company or an LLP or simply start their incorporation process by logging into the Startup India portal. (https://www.startupindia.gov.in/)
- If they decide to incorporate through the traditional method, they must ensure compliance to the below-mentioned requirements,

1. It is mandatory for directors to have a PAN number, DIN and DSC for initiating the incorporation process.
2. Approval of the name is the next step wherein the name is sent to the Registrar of Companies who decides on its validity.
3. Then, in case of a Private Limited Co., an AoA and MoA of the company is filed to the Registrar of Companies and in case of an LLP, an

LLP agreement entered between the members is filed.

4. Then, a PAN card number and Bank Account on the incorporation's name is set up for the functioning of the organization.

Essential documents

- <u>Founders Agreement-</u> This Agreement describes the relationship between the founders of the Company including the basic communication procedures, division of duties and the conflict-resolution process.
- <u>Non-Disclosure Agreement-</u> A start-up shall enter into such an agreement to ensure that whoever they provide confidential information to while entering into business with them does not disclose it to another party for a specific period of time stipulated in the Agreement.
- <u>Limited Liability Clause in an Agreement-</u> Usually inscribed in Agreements to ensure that for violation of certain clause such as the confidentiality clause, the Company does not take damages for violation of clauses more than stipulated in the Agreement.
- <u>Employment Agreement-</u> This Agreement highlights the terms and conditions of employees hired by a start-up in different capacities. It includes terms dealing with remuneration, probationary period, duties and responsibilities of employees, dispute resolution, etc.
- <u>Non-Solicitation Agreement-</u> This agreement can be entered separately or as a clause in another

agreement. Its purpose is to put a restriction on the employees from directly/indirectly soliciting or enticing an employee, customer or client to terminate his/her contract with the start-up or to motivate him to bring their business elsewhere to another party. Under Indian law, a post-termination non-solicitation agreement is not permitted however while in employment, this agreement can be entered into.

- <u>Employee handbook-</u> This handbook mentions information about the standardized rules and regulations for the company for the aid of the employee. In the handbook, the employer shall mention information relevant for employees in accordance with the national and state laws of our country applicable for employees. It includes information such as employee benefits, maternity leave, leave policies, code of conduct, sexual harassment policies, etc.
- <u>Master Agreements-</u> A start-up enters into business agreements with a lot of secondary players since they cannot perform every function in their own capacity. There shall be a master agreement which is entered between the start-up and such players which shall mention the essential terms of the scope of work and their corresponding payments along with other essential clauses for the protection of the start-up such as rights and duties of both parties, Intellectual property protection, Dispute Resolution, Termination, etc.
- <u>Specifications of the Product-</u> Specific to drone start-ups, certain regulatory requirements under the Draft UAS Rules, 2020 require individuals dealing with drones to submit exact specifications of their UAS and products to the DGCA for them

to grant approval. For instance, the Draft Rules require manufacturers of drones are required to submit the specifications and details of their UAS to the DGCA so they can be certain that the built of the product complies with the requirements prescribed by them. After this only, the manufacturer is granted the Certificate of Manufacture by the DGCA. Therefore, it is advisable for such start-ups to always be prepared with their technical and other specifications in order to deal with various regulatory compliances.

B. <u>IPR</u>

For any start-up, business, Intellectual Property Rights (IPR) are one of the most important assets that they have. They give the creator an exclusive right for the usage of their product. Drones being a developing industry, the start-ups can use these rights in their favour to increase their profits even make a name in the sector.

Being an early developer of drones, any start-up would want to excel and be recognised of their efforts in the industry. IPR is one of the best ways to achieve that goal. It increases the value of the business as well as the products like the types of drones, generate goodwill, stand against the competition, and increase revenue through licensing.

The following IPs are generally required for any start-up/ business to function:

- Trademarks

- done for names, logos, design that represents the goods or services of one start up and differentiate it to another.
- Drones are given names which can be trademarked to protect and identify the product.
- Patents
- This is for any invention the business does which could either include a new produce or a new process of doing an existing thing.
- With drones, it can be used to protect inventions with regards to parts of drones to the design making it more efficient etc.
- Copyrights
- Used to protect the work of authors/ artists/ originator.

- Industrial Designs and
- Under this right, the protection is given to any shape configuration, ornament applied by way of industrial process or manually which can be recognised by the eyes.
- Any change in design solely can be protected here. In case the design is of use for the functionality of the product or creates new product or process that will be protected under the patent's act.
- Trade Secrets.
- Any confidential information which gives the business an edge over its competitors is protected under trade secret.
- This could include any information which makes the drones of the start-up more efficient than others by way of designing, coding, products used etc.

It is of utmost importance that a start-up working in the drones' industry must have their patent, industrial design, trademark and trade secret protected. A company can consult a lawyer specialising in the field to get the best result for the protection of their rights.

C. <u>Support from Government and Financial institutes.</u>

- <u>Make In India</u>- It was launched by the government in 2014 to ease investment, promote innovation, encourage skill development, protect intellectual property, and built the greatest manufacturing infrastructure in India.
This initiative has four pillars to support the manufacturers and promote entrepreneurship.
i. New Process: Make in India recognizes to ease the business environment by de-licensing and de-regulating the industry for the growing businesses. New initiatives are coming up under this to promote entrepreneurship.
ii. New infrastructure: to develop infrastructure for the growth of the industries. The government has started to work on the development of industrial corridors and smart cities to provide modern and facilitating infrastructure. The infrastructure of Intellectual property rights has also been upgraded to support faster registration.
iii. New Sectors: Make in India has identified 25 different sectors under this campaign. Aviation is one of the sectors. Web- Portals are made for these sectors to provide detailed information.

DIGISKY, a web-portal developed specifically for information related to unmanned aircraft.

iv. New Mindset: The government will interact with the industry as a facilitator rather than as a regulator.
Make in India encourages businesses from abroad to invest and manufacture in India. Many sectors have now opened up for foreign direct investment. Make in India has also generated employment opportunities.

- <u>Startup India</u>: is one of the several schemes under the Make in India program. It aims to build an ecosystem that promotes and develops startups through the exchange of knowledge and access to funding and thereby generating large scale employment.

Incentives under this scheme:
i. The Central Government bears all the cost of the facilitator for any number of patents. Further startups are provided an 80% reduction in the total cost of filing a patent.
ii. The government has set up a policy to provide funds through venture capital. It also encourages banks and other financial institutions to provide funds through venture capital.
iii. Startups are exempted from paying income tax for three years.
iv. Startups can apply for government tenders. The "prior experience/ turnover" requirement is not applicable for them
v. Research parks will be set up for innovators to facilitate research and development.
vi. In the case of winding up operations, the process has been made easier for startups.

- <u>Atmanirbhar Bharat Abhiyaan</u>: "It is time to become vocal for our local products and make them global" Government of India to support the economy to fight against COVID-19 came up with this Abhiyaan. Atmanirbhar Bharat was launched by Hon'ble Prime Miniter, he stated that these tough times should be used to become Atmanirbhar (self-reliant) to enable the resurgence of the Indian economy. The government came up with Unlock 1 Guidelines, to enable the resumption of economic activity while maintaining abundant caution. There are five pillars to Atmanirbhar Bharat: Economy, Infrastructure, System, Vibrant Demography, and Demand. and five phases of Atmanirbhar Bharat: Phase I- Businesses including MSMEs, Phase-II- Poor, including migrants and farmers, Phase III- Agriculture, Phase IV- New Horizons of Growth, Phase V: Government Reforms and Enablers. A special economic and comprehensive package of Rs 20 lakh crores has been introduced to cater to various sections including Micro, Small and Medium Enterprises, Laborers, Middle class, industries, etc. It is expected that Atmanirbhar Bharat Abhiyaan will also support the new businesses set under the aviation sector for the growth of the drone industry.

Other Schemes

- <u>Atal Innovation Mission (AIM)</u>: this scheme was formed under the NITI Aayog (Think Tank' of the Government of India, providing both directional and policy inputs) in 2016. The objective of this scheme is to promote a culture of innovation and entrepreneurship through world-class innovation hubs, grand challenges, start-up businesses, and other self-employed activities. It offers to cover up capital cost by granting funding of up to Rs 10 crores to startups over the five years.

- <u>Composite Loan</u>: this scheme provides sanction and disbursement of working capital and term loans together from a single agency. The scheme is operated by both banks and financial institutes. The single window scheme is made to overcome difficulties and delays faced by Micro, Small, and Medium Enterprises to start production expeditiously.
- <u>Credit Facilitation Through Bank</u>- NSIC has made association with banks to arrange for credit support for Micro, Small, and Medium Enterprises. NSIC facilitates these enterprises in accessing credit support (fund based or non-fund based limits) from the banks.
- <u>Credit Guarantee Fund Trust for Micro and Small Enterprises (CGTMSE)</u>: this scheme provides collateral-free credit to both existing and new micro and small enterprise sector. Enterprises can apply for a collateral-free loan up to a limit of 2 crore rupees.
- <u>High Risk- High Reward Research</u>: this scheme provides supports and invites new proposals and ideas which have the potential to have a paradigm-shifting influence on science and technology.
- <u>Marketing Assistance Scheme</u>: to provide financial support to Micro, Small, and Medium Enterprises so they can showcase their product or services in the prevalent market.

- <u>Pradhan Mantri MUDRA Yojana:</u> provide financial support to the microenterprise sector having loan requirements up to 10 lakh without collaterals.
- <u>Raw Material Assistance Scheme</u>: By National Small Industrial Corporation (NSIC) to help Micro, Small, and Medium Enterprises by financing the purchase of Raw material (both indigenous & imported) so they can manufacture quality products.
- <u>SIDBI Make in India Soft Loan Fund for MSMEs (SMILE):</u> aims to take forward the Make in India campaign and help finance enterprises within Micro, Small, and Medium Enterprises Sector by providing soft loans.
- <u>Stand Up India</u>: this scheme provides bank loans to at least one SC/ST borrower and at least one woman per bank branch, of between 10 lakh to 1 crore rupees to set up an enterprise in manufacturing, services, or trading sector.
- <u>Start-up Research Grant</u>: by science and engineering research board to assist researchers in initiating their research career in frontier areas of science and engineering to establish themselves. Research grant of Rs 30 Lakh Plus overheads for two years.
- <u>Support for International Patent Protection in Electronics and Information Technology(SIP-EIT):</u> this scheme provides financial support to Micro, Small and Medium Enterprises, and technology startups for international patent filing.

D. <u>Development in drone investment in 2019 and 2020 outlook</u>

1. Drone Investment in 2019:

- In 2019 $1.2 billion was invested into the drone industry. The total investment of 2019 broke last year's record.
- A large portion of investment came from the Venture Capital investment, with $830 million invested.
- Over the years, a total of $4.443 has been invested in the drone market.
- In 2020, we can expect continued growth in the drone market.

2. Passenger drones Companies are coming in

- This year we have four different sectors in the drone industry: drone, passenger drone, counter-drone, and UTM companies. Investment in passenger drone companies is the highest in 2019 among the four sectors.
- All these four sectors are currently seen at a different maturity stage and are likely to experience different technological and regulatory hurdles.
- It is expected that passenger drones will be subjected to the strictest rules and regulations, as well as the highest technological hurdles as they will be carrying humans.
- This sector will increase popularly in the year 2020 not only we will see a rise in the number of passenger drone concepts, but also government funding for smart city and Urban Air Mobility initiatives.

3. Drone delivery companies

- In 2020 we can expect an increase in the number of investments by the drone delivery companies, as the market is expanding in terms of the scale of operations.

4. M&As

- M&As are becoming a form of expansion of company operation, companies are using it as a growth model.
- M&As will continue to be a trend in 2020 for large companies to expand geographically and for creating new and improved solutions for their clients.

5. Continuous growth

- The research has shown that the drone market is continuously growing vertically and signs of significant horizontal growth as well. The market is spreading across the globe.
- There is also an increasing number of drone companies venture into partnerships with non-drone companies to provide new and unique solutions.
- In 2020, we see continuous growth in the Indian market for drones.

II. CHAPTER 4

LAWS GOVERNING DRONES IN INDIA

A. Current Laws

The basic law governing drones starts from the Aircraft Rules, where *Rule 15A* governs the Operations of the RPAS. Under this rule, the regulatory framework was issued by the DGCA as a *CAR, under Section 3- Air transport, Series X, Part I, Issue I*. This was brought in by the DGCA in the year 2018, which legalized and regulated the use of drones in India. Consequently, the developments started to begin. Under the chairmanship of the Minister of Civil Aviation, a drone task force was constituted. This was done to liberalize the regime and tap into more potential uses of drones, particularly in the commercial sector. The task force came up with the Drone Ecosystem Policy Roadmap in 2019. Subsequently, several new initiatives were launched by the authorities focused on capacity building of the drone ecosystem in 2019 and this trend continued in 2020 also.

The authorities are following a more evidence-based regulatory approach whereby they invited companies to conduct experiments and provide proof of concepts like Beyond Visual Line of Sight (BVLOS) in 2019-2020. This was with the intent to enhance the drone industry by providing more regulations for enhanced drone operations. Various companies like Swiggy, Zomato and TATA have also submitted their applications with the

DGCA to conduct experiments BVLOS for the purposes of delivery of customer products.

In 2019, the Ministry of Civil Aviation, also introduced guidelines, National Counter Rogue Drone Guidelines (NCRD Guidelines), as with the advent of developments within the drone industry there also have been cases of rogue drones, India has estimated around 6 lakhs rogue drones and unregulated UAVs of various sizes and capacities. To handle the above scenario the Ministry of Civil Aviation has suggested a counter-rogue drone deployment plan, categorized across three models, based on the sensitivity of vital assets and installations.

These guidelines can be deployed to address the relevant threats effectively.

The strategic installations differ from state to state and place to place, based on their geographical condition, criticality and construction type but standard categorization would be:

Full-scale model:
- It will work for the protection of vital assets of critical national importance like Rashtrapati Bhawan, Parliament House, nuclear installations, major airports, etc.
- Counter-Unmanned Aircraft System (C-UAS) with primary and passive detection means like radar, Radio Frequency (RF) detectors, electro-optical, and infrared cameras to be installed.

Mid-segment model:

- It will protect installations like metro airports, oil refineries, ports, and power plants, etc.
- A lower level of threat mitigation techniques (compared to the full-scale model) to be installed with Counter-Unmanned Aircraft System (C-UAS).

Basic model:

- Aims to protect state secretariats, important official premises, monuments of national importance etc.
- The basic threat mitigation technology to be used.

   A realistic vulnerability analysis of identified vital areas/vital points by specialist security agencies based on impact assessment from a different category of drones, natural camouflage, and local security scenario would help to establish Counter-Unmanned Aircraft System (C-UAS).

The Counter-Unmanned Aircraft System (C-UAS) includes the following modern weapons:

- *Sky Fence:* It aims to block a lethal drone that uses a range of signal disruptors to jam the flight path and prevent them from entering their target, a sensitive installation or event venue.
- *Drone gun:* It is capable of jamming the radio, a global positioning system (GPS) and a mobile signal between the drone and the pilot. Further, it forces the drone to the ground in good time before it could wreak any damage.
- *Advanced Test High Energy Asset (ATHENA):* It works by firing a high energy laser beam on a rogue drone resulting in its complete destruction in the air. It is a very costly technology and is currently being tested by the US army.
- *Drone Catcher:* It swiftly approaches an enemy drone and grabs it by throwing a net around it.

Such a tool is required when a rogue drone is needed to be captured safely to extract incriminating evidence from it

- *Skywall 100:* It is the ground version of the 'drone catcher' and it works by bringing down a UAV use parachute that is hurled through a net from 100 meters distance.

  On January 6, 2020, the Ministry of Defence, launched a web portal for providing No Objection Certificate (NOC). This is for undertaking an aerial survey with the final permission of DGCA. The portal will be used by various vendors engaged by state governments/public sector undertakings/ autonomous bodies in seeking NOC from MoD. Through this initiative, the MoD will be able to reduce the time usually taken in issuing NOC and will ensure expeditious disposal of applications for carrying out aerial surveys and/ or remote sensing surveys.

Thereafter, when several instances of non-compliant UAS being flown came to the notice of the government, they issued two public notices one on 13th January 2020 and another one 8th June 2020, seeking voluntary disclosure of unregulated drones. As per the notice, persons in possession of such non-compliant drones can submit the required information/ voluntary disclosure through an online portal (Digital Sky). The drone enlistment form for voluntary disclosure has two parts. After uploading the drone owner's information, the owner will receive an Ownership Acknowledgement Number (OAN). Using the OAN, the owner will upload the drone-related information and will receive a Drone Acknowledgement Number (DAN). Each drone will require a fresh enlistment.

i. **Penalties for Non-Compliance under the current laws:**

In the case of violation of the CAR, the following penalties may be imposed:

o an operator's Unique Identification Number (UIN) or Unmanned Aircraft Operator Permit (UOAP) issued by the DGCA may be suspended or cancelled.

Breach of compliance to any of the requirements of the CAR and falsification of records or documents may attract penal action, including the imposition of penalties as per the Indian Penal Code 1860 (IPC), which includes but is not limited to:

- *Section 287:* negligent conduct with respect to machinery (carrying a maximum sentence of imprisonment that may extend to six months or a fine that may extend up to 1,000 Indian rupees, or both);
- *Section 336:* act endangering life or personal safety of others (carrying a maximum sentence of imprisonment that may extend to three months or a fine that may extend to 250 rupees, or both);
- *Section 337:* causing hurt by an act endangering the life or personal safety of others (carrying a maximum sentence of imprisonment that may extend to six months or a fine that may extend to 500 rupees, or both);
- *Section 338:* causing grievous hurt by an act endangering the life or personal safety of others

(carrying a maximum sentence of imprisonment that may extend to two years or a fine that may extend to 1,000 rupees, or both); or
- any other relevant section of the IPC.

Penalties for contravention or failure to comply with any rules or directions issued under Rule 133A of the Aircraft Rules 1939 (the rule under which CARs are issued), are punishable to the extent of imprisonment for a term not exceeding six months or a fine not exceeding 200,000 rupees or both.

Apart from these, the DGCA additionally also has issued a _Flying Training Circular_ dated 30th January 2019, which gives out the procedures for the training of a Remote Pilot and applies to all the approved Flying Training organizations (FTOs) who are imparting training on remote pilots.

And a _RPAS Guidance Material_, latest revised on 11th March 2020. The aim of this was to acquaint the public with the intricacies of the system and help them understand the process of acquiring the operator permit, the UIN and other related things, in a better manner. The guidance material is quite detailed and is drafted in an easily understandable language.

Despite having all these regulatory frameworks in place, the Ministry of Civil Aviation is in the process of bringing separate rules, called as _Unmanned Aircraft System (UAS) Rules, 2020_. They have already published a draft on their website, and are awaiting public challenges and suggestions on the same. After which, they will publish a finalized version of the rules, this is probably expected to be done by September 2020. This will be one step further from the existing framework, as the CARs are less effective, and having these Rules in place will help make the framework more stringent, as they have in the Rules also, introducing new penalties than just the IPC provisions. Moreover, with the introduction of these rules, the existing policies governing drones will no longer be effective and the UAS Rules will replace them, pursuant to which, DGCA will be able to make more CARs to fill in the gaps.

B. <u>Draft UAS rules 2020</u>

In June 2020, The Ministry of Civil Aviation notified the Draft Unmanned Aviation System (UAS) Rules, 2020. These rules are in continuation of the regulation, which was issued in 2018. With these rules, the government aims to regulate the manufacture, import, trade, ownership, establishment drone ports, and the operation of the Unmanned Aircraft System. The word drone is given the terminology- Unmanned Aircraft (UA). Under the draft rules, they have subcategorized the UA as – Remotely Piloted Aircraft, Autonomous Aircraft, and Model Aircraft. The definitions of all these terminologies have been provided under *Rule* 2. Remotely Piloted Aircraft has further been divided into five categories based on their weight; Nano: less than or equal to 250 grams, Micro: from 250 grams to 2kg, Small: From 2 kg to 25 kg, Medium: from 25 kg to 150 kg, Large: greater than 150 kg.

These Draft Rules are independent of the Aircraft Rules, 2937. The Draft Rules have been established under Section 4, 5 and 8 of the Aircraft Act, 1934 and the Civil Aviation Requirements were established under Rule 133A of the Aircraft Rules, 1937, these CARs are subservient to the Aircraft Rules, 1937. *Rule 1(4)* of the Draft Rules states that provisions of Aircraft Rules, 1937 won't apply on UAS and matters connected therewith, unless specifically provided in the draft rules. As the provision, the CARs on drone regulation will cease to exist once the final rules are published by the MOCA. The Government through its regulations shows that they want the drones as an independent industry and not just as an extension of the conventional aviation industry.

The government has also taken initiative to take challenges and suggestions on these draft rules. The government should take note of these comments and try to incorporate the changes in the final UAS, Rules, 2020.
Following are the links for the DGCA website and the online platform (Digital Sky):

➤ https://dgca.gov.in/digigov-portal/

Tabular representation UAS Drones as per Draft Rules 2020

Category	Nano	Micro	Small	Medium	Large

All-Up Weight (Including Payload)	Less Than Or Equal To 250 Gram	Greater Than 250 Gram And Less Than Or Equal To 2 Kilogram	Greater Than 2 Kilograms And Less Than Or Equal To 25 Kilogram	Greater Than 25 Kilograms And Less Than Or Equal To 150 Kilogram	Greater Than 150 Kilogram
Unique Identification Number	Yes	Yes	Yes	Yes	Yes
Unmanned Aircraft Operator Permit	No	Yes	Yes	Yes	Yes
NPNT Compliance	No	Yes	Yes	Yes	Yes
Flight Plan	No	Yes	Yes	Yes	Yes
Pilot License	No	Yes	Yes	Yes	Yes

C. <u>Online platform</u>

➢ Link to the digital Sky Platform: https://digitalsky.dgca.gov.in/

i. Digital Sky Platform and its hurdles

- In 2018, the DGCA introduced Drone Regulations 1.0 (CAR 1.0), which was the first policy to govern the usage of civic drones in India.
- In pursuance to these Regulations, the DGCA also promised setting up of a Digital Sky platform through which the authorities would get a clear view about the drones operating in the air as all required permissions, permits, licenses, etc would function through this single platform.
- However, till date, it is not fully operational in nature and it is yet to be developed. This is leading to a standstill of operations and causing hindrance to the development of the drone industry. The text of the policy is not criticized but its slow and undeveloped execution is. The Digital sky platform is since its beginning, in a beta phase which simply is accepting applications such as Unique Identification Number, Drone registration and Unmanned Aircraft Operator Permits.
- The vision of having a comprehensive online platform is not yet achieved since there is no automated system as of now that is designed for functions such as authorities giving permission to drones to fly or for them to monitor its flight paths and its functioning.
- The Hurdles to the platform begin right at the beginning of the Registration Process for the Digital Sky platform. The website often shows no response since it has a bad UX and is error stricken. Then, comes the struggle of acquiring permits, certificates and licenses. This is a tiresome process for businesses because various permissions are required from different ministries.

- All drone applicants whether owners or operators are required to get an ETA approval, from the wireless planning and coordination wing within the Department of telecommunications. But if someone wants to imports drones and its compartments from abroad, they need to procure approval from the DGCA in the form of an import license. After this process, there is a requirement of security clearance from the Ministry of
- Home affairs to get UINs. Then, for categories other than Nano drones, operators/owners are then also required to apply for UAOPs (operator permit).
- Besides the procedural hurdles for operators and owners, the drone manufacturers are also required to comply with certain technical requirements wherein their drones shall match the minimum essential hardware design features set up by the DGCA. Most of the drone providers in India are foreign entities that are unable to comply with such local designs.
- This form of regulation under CAR 1.0 was highly exhaustive and strict in nature and completely negated the vision of a single-window platform. While government operations of drones are often free from such hurdles, drone developing startups and companies often face challenges.
- The reasons cited for its failure is the cancellation of various tenders entered with companies designed to maintain and develop the Digital sky platform. Another reason was the non-availability of air space date from multiple states leading to the failure of categorizing the air space into

- green, yellow and red zones. This leads to hurdles in grant of automated permissions.
- With the coming up of UAS rules, 2020, it was believed that some of these hurdles would be taken care of, however, even under the new rules, under its schedule, I (Requirements for obtaining Authorisation as importer, manufacturer, trader, owner or operator), Clearance from several departments such as Ministry of Home Affairs, Ministry of Broadcasting, Ministry of Defence ("MoD"), MoCA and DGCA is still required. Therefore, still, no single window approval system is provided. Also, there is still no visible possibility yet to create an automated system which governs flight plans, permissible zones, proper security procedures, etc.

ii. Recent Developments in the Digital Sky Platform

- The platform still has a long way to go however, there are some positive steps taken by the Ministry of Civil Aviation towards its development.
- Chairman of the Ministry of Civil Aviation, Amber Dubey announced In September 2019, that by October 2nd, 2020, the first phase of the Digital sky platform will go live. The platform would be updated to provide flight clearances for drone operations in India finally.
- He also stated, that by then, the platform would also integrate with other government entities, allow management of airspace workflows, plan drone flights and log post-flight data submissions along with other developments. Therefore, from October, only NPNT compliant drones would be able to operate in the Indian airspace as mandated in the Draft Rules.

- He also stated that the platform has already started with certain developments. For instance, the yellow zones have been activated on the platform. While green zones are still being prepared.
- Also, recently in July 2020, Quidich Innovations Labs and Asteria Aerospace (Indian Companies) collaborated to ensure the flight of India's first NPNT compliant flight enabled through the Digital Sky platform. The flight was carried out in the green zone as notified by the DGCA on the platform. The entire process was validated through the digital sky portal which showed that the platform is started to develop.
- It is true that the platform still isn't fully operational and has a long way to go in terms of getting automatic flight clearances or in the development of a single-window system, among other things. But as ensured by the Ministry of Civil Aviation, the developments shall be ready by October 2020.

III. <u>CHAPTER 5</u>

<u>COMPARISON</u>

A. <u>A comparison of the Draft UAS Rules, 2020 and the CAR on RPAS, 2018</u>

- *Rule 1* of UAS Draft Rules mentions applicability of the Rules to the whole of India as well as extra – territorial application, whereas CAR does not.
- Many new terms have been introduced in the draft rules as compared to CAR.
- The classification has stayed the same in both, with the only difference being that the category changes from Nano to Micro with the speed and height of the UAS.
- The authorisation has been introduced along with UAN.
- In the rules, an importer needs clearance for 'parts or components' as well. The certificate of manufacture is also introduced only in the rules.
- Inspection and safety oversight has been introduced in the rules, the power of the same is with the DGCA.
- CAR and Rules both mention laboratories for certifying/ testing, however, the list has not been uploaded on the DGCA website yet.
- Exemptions have been put for Micro category as well in the rules. CAR had exempted Nano and Micro category from certain specifications. Emergency recovery system is also newly introduced in the rules.
- Maintenance has now become mandatory under the rules.

- Under the rules, it is the duty of the importer or the manufacturer to apply for UIN. Nano category is also not exempted from the same.
- In cases of change in ownership or loss, CAR allowed for cancellation of UIN in comparison to deregistration under the rules.
- Transfer is prohibited unless done by an authorised person.
- A permit is required under both which is non-transferable. However, under the rules, Nano class is excluded.
- Three categories of trained pilots have been put in the rules.
- Rules are much stricter in putting restrictions over a UAS in flight. However, at the same time carrying of hazardous material has been allowed with permission under the rules.
- Privacy has been included in both CAR and rules. Further suggestions have been made to have stricter implementations of the privacy laws of the country.
- Both have safety flying requirements however, rules do not specify any meteorological conditions for flying or safety risk assessments or designated safe areas.
- Rules introduced the new concept of drone ports and drone corridors.
- UTM has been introduced in the rules to manage air traffic. This will also ensure integration with the existing air traffic systems. UTM is essential for BVLOS and thus helping in smooth running of those UAS as well.
- DGCA has the power to detain part(s) of the UAS under the rules.

- Third-party insurance is mandatory under both. Insurance is very specific under the rules however general under CAR.
- DGCA has been given the power to issue CARs for the rules. DGCA also has the power to suspend/ cancel/ revoke the license under both. Under the rules, however, the right to be heard is given before cancellation. Even the power to inspect has been broadened under the rules.
- CAR gave penalties under IPC, however same is not mentioned under the rules. Rules allow for defence for 'unavoidable circumstance' which is not defined, defence was not given under CAR.
- Natural justice is followed under the rules and thus in the process appeals are allowed under the rules.
- The rules are overall much stricter in application than CAR. Power of the DGCA has been increased while also keeping a check on it. New terms have also been introduced.

B. <u>Comparison of Indian drone regulation with other countries</u>

- Rules and regulations around the world for drones are still in their infancy. India has the opportunity to move ahead and lead the initiative to protect its interests and make laws which also do not hamper the security implications of the world in the country.
- Internationally, ICAO has been the platform to formulate rules for drone operations. Work was started in 2007. RPAS manual - Circular 328 in 2011, became the first step to regulate the sector. It called for comments to develop SARPs, with the

- aim to support Procedures for Air Navigation Services (PANS) and guidance material to harmonise laws for safe and seamless operation of drones around the world.
- Seeing the potential of the drones' industry, many agencies, companies, countries have started to develop laws for the sector.
- European aviation safety agency (EASA) is making regulations on behalf of the EC for drone operations. "The EASA published a comprehensive proposal in May 2017 covering the technical and operational aspects of operating drones."
- All UAVs above 250 grams have to be registered. Even though EASA is formulating laws, it is on individual countries to set
- +restrictions. Each European country has its own standard of restrictions and the strictness depends from one country to another.
- For example: "one can fly drones commercially in Switzerland if line-of-sight can be ensured, within certain altitude limitations and not flying near protected areas such as airports. On the other hand, France has somewhat more restrictive regulations in place and it is mandated that any drone operation over the city of Paris needs to be authorised by aviation authorities."
- Ethics, regulation and implementation in the drone's industry are topics for open and more advanced conversations. The laws also need to be updated at the speed of advancement in the industry.
- Laws and policies need to be binding in nature for effective implementation.

- "According to 6Wresearch (Market Research and Consulting firm), the Indian UAV market is poised to grow at a CAGR of 18% during 2017 – 23 in terms of revenue".
- Usage in the military is far more than in commercial in India, however the same is predicted to be changed.
- Infrastructure and agriculture are expected to see the most growth.
- Poland was the first country in 2013 to have established all special regulatory frameworks, including both VLOS and BVLOS.
- 63 nations have some regulations for drones already in place, 9 have pending regulations and 5 have temporarily banned the usage.
- ISO has drafted the first-ever global standards for drone operations, called Draft International Standard for Unmanned Aircraft Systems Operation. They are not mandatory in nature and establish the no-fly zones.
- It also formulates uniform industry regulations for drone technology to ensure safety and security.
- Three other standards focus on technical specification, manufacturing quality and traffic management.

IV. CHAPTER 6

UAS RULES SIMPLIFIED

I. Definitions

- **Autonomous Aircraft** – a subcategory of a UAS, which does not require pilot intervention for its operations and flies with the help of the pre-installed program.
- **Autonomous operation** – includes operation of an autonomous aircraft (defined above)
- **Beyond Visual Line of Sight Operation**- BVLOS is an operation of a UAS where the remote pilot has no direct view of the aircraft while operating it.
- **Certificate of manufacture** – issued by DGCA to an authorised manufacturer and importer to certify that their product design meets the standards under the rules.
- **Command and Control Link** – for operating the UAS, there has to be a connection established between the remote pilot and the UAS for smooth functioning.
- **Controlled Airspace** - defined dimension within which UAS traffic management service will be provided.
- **Danger Area** – airspace over which operating the UAS will be considered dangerous at a certain time.
- **Drone Corridor**- airspace segregated specifically for the operation of UAS from manned aircraft.
- **Drone port** – an airport for UAS.
- **Geo-fencing** –Geo-fencing is a virtual barrier created using a combination of the GPS (Global Positioning System) network and Local Radio

Frequency connections such as Wi-Fi or Bluetooth. It is used to determine the geographical boundaries of UAS operations.

- **Maintenance** – ensuring that the UAS remains compliant both technically and physically with the rules throughout its lifetime
- **Model Remote Piloted Aircraft system** – type of UAS used for educational and recreational purposes, to be only flown within visual line of sight.
- **Payload**– addition to the original body of the UAS which is detachable and is not necessary for its control.
- **Prohibited Area-** defined areas over which flying of UAS is not allowed at any time under any circumstances.
- **Recreational Flying** -Flying off the UAS simply for the pleasure and enjoyment of the Pilot. Does not include any commercial purpose.
- **Remote Pilot** – a person on the ground who operates the UAS during flight.
- **Remotely Piloted Aircraft** – a UAS flown by a remote pilot
- **Remotely piloted Aircraft system** – a system consisting of all requirements to fly a RPA.
- **Remote pilot station** – equipment used by a remote pilot to operate UAS.
- **Restricted Area** – defined areas over which flying of UAS is restricted.
- **Remotely Piloted Aircraft observer** – person assisting the remote pilot for the safe operation of the UAS
- **Unmanned Aircraft**– a category of aircraft which is operated without a pilot on board

- **<u>Unmanned Aircraft System</u>** – a system consisting of all the elements to operate a UA
- **<u>UAS Traffic Management</u>**- equivalent to Air Traffic Control for UAS
- **<u>Visual Line of Sight operations</u>**-The operator or the observer shall always keep the unmanned aircraft in their direct view while operating the UA

II. Applicability

The UAS Rules apply to all persons engaged with the drone industry in India including owners, operators, importers, manufacturers, traders of UAS and those involved in its leasing, transferring and maintenance. The applicability of the UAS rules extends to UAS registered in India. They also apply to UAS operating outside the Indian territory if they are registered in India.

III. Categorization

UAS is categorized into three categories under the UAS Rules, 2020:

A. Remotely Piloted Aircraft System- Flown from a remote pilot station
B. Model Remotely Piloted Aircraft System- Used for educational or experimental purposes and is flown only within visual line of sight
C. Autonomous Unmanned Aircraft System- Flown without any intervention from a pilot in its management and flight

IV. Classification

The UAS Rule, 2020 classifies UAS according to its Maximum All-up-weight (including payload). These are the following types,

i.   Nano: Less than or equal to 250 gram;
ii. Micro: Greater than 250 gram and less than or equal to 2 kilograms;
iii. Small: Greater than 2 kilograms and less than or equal to 25 kilograms;
iv. Medium: Greater than 25 kilograms and less than or equal to 150 kilograms;
v.   Large: Greater than 150 kilograms.

Further, the category of Nano UAS will be reclassified into Micro Drones if it exceeds the maximum speed to more than 15 meters/second or its maximum attainable height to more than 15 meters and range to more than 100 meters.

V. Authorization

Under the UAS Rules, 2020, all persons associated with the drone industry in India shall get authorized by the DGCA including importers, manufacturers, Traders, owners, operators to act in their particular capacities in India. They shall be authorized as an **Authorized Person** under the rules by applying to the DGCA through the digital sky platform.

Process

1. Eligibility
To be eligible for such authorization, the pre-requisite is that the applicant shall be one of the following,

- An individual who is a citizen of India and is 18 or above in age.
- A company or a corporate body having its principal place of business within India or its chairman or two-thirds of its directors being citizens of India. Further, whose substantial ownership and effective control vests with Indian nationals through it.
- A firm or association of persons or body of individuals or a local authority or any legal entity, or Central and state government or an agency, provided that their substantial ownership and effective control vests with Indian nationals.

2. Unique Authorization Number (UAN)

- If the Eligibility criteria is met, then an application is to be submitted as per the manner and procedure prescribed under Schedule I of the Draft Rules to the DGCA.
- After which, the DGCA, if satisfied with the application will grant a Unique Authorization Number (UAN) to the applicant to act as an authorized UAS importer, manufacture, owner, operator or trader.
- This authorization shall be valid for a period specified by the DGCA and if not, then for a maximum period of 5 years.
- The applicant can also apply for renewal in the same manner and procedure prescribed under Schedule I. Additionally, the eligibility criteria given above shall also be met. The validity of the renewal shall be the period specified by the DGCA and if not, then for a maximum period of 5 years.

*It is pertinent to note that foreign individuals are not entitled to apply for 'authorization' under the UAS Rules. Additionally, for foreign companies, they can only be authorized if their substantial ownership and effective control vests with Indian nationals.

VI. Import

- An authorized importer shall first make an application to the DGCA for import clearance in the manner and procedure prescribed under Schedule II of the UAS Rules on the Digital Sky platform.
- The DGCA on being satisfied, recommends the application to the Directorate General of foreign trade who determines whether an import clearance shall be issued or not.
- One of the pre-requisites of importation of UAS in India is that the authorized importer shall procure a Certificate of Manufacture before applying to the DGCA for import clearance, the procedure for which is explained below.

VII. Manufacturing

- Under the UAS rules, every authorised importer and authorised manufacturer of UAS or its parts and components shall first procure a 'Certificate of Manufacturer'. This certificate ensures that the design of the UAS meets the requirements and specifications mentioned under the UAS Rules and is applicable for all categories of UAS, including Nano.
- The DGCA shall appoint testing laboratories or organizations that shall be responsible for ensuring

that the authorized manufacturers' or importers' products are in compliance with the manufacturing requirements under Schedule II.

- The list of such testing centres shall then be published by the DGCA in the Digital Sky platform for the purpose of awareness of the applicants.
- Additionally, all manufacturing units are subjected to safety and oversight operations by the DGCA.

Process

- The applicant is first required to make an application in the manner and

procedure prescribed under Schedule II. The applicant can give a preference for training centres suited to them. After which, the DGCA shall allot a training centre to them.
- The applicant shall then submit all the specifications and details of their UAS to the centre to show that their UAS is in compliance with the requirements prescribed under Schedule II the rules.
- If the requirements are met, the centre submits a test report to the DGCA based on which, the DGCA grants the Certificate of Manufacture to the applicant.

Equipment Type Approval

- One of the pre-requisites for this Certificate of Manufacture is that the applicant shall first procure an 'equipment type approval' (ETA) from the Wireless Planning and Coordination (WPC) wing of the Department of Telecommunications. This is an approval granted to allow the operation of drones in de-licensed frequency bands as well as for details of emergency recovery systems.

VIII.   Maintenance

- Every UAS in India shall be maintained in accordance to the requirements given under the UAS Rules in order to operate in India.
- Every UAS manufacturer or importer is obligated to maintain a maintenance manual which he is required to provide as part of mandatory sale documents to authorised traders, owners or operators.
- This manual shall include maintenance requirements and procedures. Manufacturer or importers shall also be obligated to provide training to the personnel involved in such maintenance.
- The authorized importer or manufacturer can also set up authorized maintenance centres which shall work on the procedures set up in the maintenance manual and shall consist of trained personnel.
- They are obligated to notify the DGCA who shall be authorized to carry out safety and oversight over these centres.
- The owner, traders, and operators on the receiving end of these maintenance manuals shall ensure that their UAS is being maintained in accordance with the manuals and shall maintain a record of such maintenance.

IX. Identification of UAS

- For a UAS to be operated or owned in India, they shall be allotted a Unique Identification Number (UIN) by the DGCA.
- For obtaining a UIN, an authorized Manufacturer or Importer is required to file an application to the DGCA in the manner and procedure prescribed under Schedule III of the UAS Rules.
- The DGCA shall on being satisfied with the validity of the application shall then grant a UIN to the UAS which shall be affixed on the UAS in a visible and identifiable manner.

X. Ownership, Transfer, Sale and Lease of UAS

- Only an Authorized owner can own a UAS or its part or component in India and only an Authorized Trader shall engage in buying, selling, or leasing of UAS in India.
- A UAS can only be transferred, sold, or leased from one authorised person to another in the manner and procedure prescribed under Schedule IV of the UAS Rules.
- If it is to be done in any other manner as prescribed in the preceding point, it shall be authorized by the DGCA

Obligation on the Owner of UAS to notify to the DGCA

- A registered owner of a UAS is obligated to notify to the DGCA in the manner prescribed by them in case of any transfer of ownership by him, if a UAS ceases to be owned by them if the UAS is damaged or beyond repair and if there has been a loss of UAS or it has been announced missing.

- On being satisfied with the presence of any of the above-mentioned situations, the UIN of the UAS shall be deregistered by the DGCA.

XI. Acceptance of Non-Compliant UAS

- A non-compliant UAS imported or manufactured in India on or before the date specified by the Central Government (the date of enactment of the Draft UAS Rules) can be accepted by the DGCA in the manner and procedure prescribed under Schedule V.
- A compliant UAS is one which has been granted a UIN by the DGCA and which meets the manufacturing requirements prescribed under the UAS rules as explained under Part VI of this chapter.

XII. Operator Permit, Pilot License and Training Institutes Requirements

General requirements

- UAS are only permitted to fly in permissible areas identified on the digital sky platform.
- No imported or manufactured UAS other than a compliant UAS shall be operated in India.
- UAS shall only be operated by an authorized operator. They can be assisted by a qualified remote pilot, wherever required under the rules.

UAS Operator Permit (UAOP)

- Only an authorized UAS Operator is permitted to operate a UAS in India.
- Every UAS operator (except for the Nano category) shall procure a permit in the manner

and procedure prescribed under Schedule VI of the UAS rules by the DGCA. The operating conditions of the UAS shall be prescribed by the DGCA in the permit issued by them.

- The validity period of this permit shall be 5 years maximum.
- Renewal of this permit can also be permitted in the same manner and procedure prescribed under Schedule VI of the UAS rules by the DGCA for a period not exceeding 5 years at a time.

Qualified Remote Pilot

- No person other than a Qualified Remote Pilot (QEP) shall be authorised to operate a Micro UAS. For Nano category of UAS, no such requirement exists.
- The requirements for such qualification is mentioned under Schedule VII of the UAS Rules. The Pilot shall be 18 years of age, passed the tenth standard and must have undergone training as specified under the UAS Rules and shall be discussed below.
- Other than the Nano and Micro category of UAS, for any higher category of UAS, the Pilot shall firstly be a Qualified Remote Pilot and secondly, he shall obtain a Remote Pilot's License. (RPL)
- The DGCA shall grant this license as per the manner and procedure prescribed under Schedule VII of the Draft Rules.
- For foreign pilots, an additional security clearance shall be issued by the Ministry of Home Affairs in addition to being a Qualified Remote Pilot and having a Remote Pilot's License.

Training Requirements

- Additionally, the Qualified Remote Pilot (applicable for Micro category of UAS and above) is also obligated to undergo training from an authorised training institute as specified under Schedule VII of the UAS Rules.

- An application shall be submitted by the institute to the DGCA as per the manner and procedure prescribed under Schedule VII based on which, they grant authorization to them.
- This authorisation shall be valid for a period specified by the DGCA or for the maximum period of 5 years and can be renewed every 5 years in the same manner and procedure prescribed under Schedule VII.

XIII. General Conditions for Operation of UAS in India

A. <u>Permission before take-off</u>- No UAS shall fly in India unless permission has been granted by the DGCA through the Digital Sky platform in the manner and procedure prescribed by the DGCA. Along with this, the operator, pilot or observer flying the UAS shall ensure that the UAS remains within the area of for which permission was obtained. They are also obligated to maintain a log of the flight and furnish through the Digital sky platform.

B. <u>Non-operation areas</u>- No person shall be authorized to fly their UAS over any of the areas specified under Schedule VIII. These areas include airport areas, Danger Areas, Defence areas, sea and coast lines, etc. The Central Government is permitted to allow government agencies or airport operators to fly over these restricted areas under exceptional circumstances.

C. <u>Privacy-</u> While flying of the UAS, imagery can be captured by it but not in the non-permissible areas. (Permissible area is the one the owner have been granted to operate their UAS in by the DGCA). And while capturing such imagery, the UAS operator or pilot shall ensure that the privacy of individuals and their property is maintained.

Additionally, one of the requirements for the grant of UAS Operator Permit under Schedule VII of the UAS Rules is that the UAS operator shall ensure the privacy of individuals and their property while operating the UAS.

D. <u>Payload and Droppage of Articles-</u> UAS regulation in India prohibits carriage of payload by any UAS, except as permitted by the DGCA. Similarly, the dropping of any articles from a UAS in motion is prohibited in India as well, except in the manner and procedure specified by the DGCA.

E. <u>Complete Prohibition on carriage of certain items-</u> Restriction placed on the carriage of arms, ammunition, munitions of war, implements of war, explosives and military stores, except as permitted by the DGCA and only in the manner and procedure prescribed by them.

F. <u>Rules of Air-</u> Every UAS operator is obligated to comply with Rules of Air that shall be issued by the DGCA in the form of CARs in the coming future.

G. <u>Insurance-</u>Every UAS in India shall have a valid third party insurance to cover the liability caused by any mishap involving the UAS that may cause death or bodily injury to another person or damage to property. The compensations scheme for such accidents shall be governed by the Motor Vehicles Act, 1988.

H. <u>Dangerous Flying</u>- It is considered dangerous flying under the UAS Rules if a person operates the UAS in a physical or mental condition, under an intoxicated state or under the influence of psychoactive substances. It is also considered dangerous flying if the person flying the UAS flies it in such proximity to another person, property, or aircraft so as to cause unnecessary damage to it/them. Such dangerous flying is prohibited.

XIV. Drone Port

- A Drone Port can be used for arrival, departure, surface movements and associated maintenance or commercial activities of UAS.

<u>Eligibility</u>

To be eligible, an applicant shall fulfil one of the following criteria,

- An individual who is a citizen of India and is 18 or above in age.
- A company or a corporate body having its principal place of business within India or it meets the equity holding criteria as specified by the Central Government from time to time.
- A firm or association of persons or body of individuals or a local authority or any legal entity, or Central and state government or an agency

Process

- If eligibility criteria is met, the applicant shall make an application in the manner and procedure prescribed under Schedule IX of the UAS Rules to the DGCA through the Digital Sky Platform for obtaining authorization or license for drone port.

- On being satisfied with the application, the DGCA shall grant the authorization or the license (for whichever the application was sought) to the applicant.
- The license for the drone port shall be granted to the applicant for a period not exceeding 5 years and can be renewed every 5 years in the same manner and procedure prescribed under Schedule IX. The grant of such license shall be subjected to the security clearance of the applicant by the DGCA if needed.
- Since the UAS Rules also prescribe an option of a grant of a temporary license for temporary operations of UAS, the authorization for Drone Port shall be granted for a period of 3 months maximum.

XV. Unmanned Aircraft System Traffic Management (UTM)

The Central Government is authorized to establish an Unmanned Aircraft Traffic Management System in the Indian Airspace for UAS operation.

UTM License

- A person intending to provide UTM Services shall file an application to the DGCA through the Digital Sky platform in the manner and procedure prescribed under Schedule X of the UAS Rules. The DGCA on being

satisfied with the application shall grant a UTM license to such person.

- The validity period for such license shall be specified by DGCA and if not, it should be valid for a maximum period of 5 years. For renewal of such license, the applicant shall file an application in the same manner and procedure prescribed under Schedule X.

UTM Personnel License

- Any person who shall engage in UTM Services in the Indian Airspace or Foreign Airspace (under any International arrangement) shall also procure a UTM personnel license by filing an application to the DGCA through the Digital Sky platform in the manner and procedure prescribed under Schedule X of the UAS Rules.
- The validity period for such license shall be specified by DGCA and if not, it should be valid for a maximum period of 5 years. For renewal of such license, the applicant shall file an application in the same manner and procedure prescribed under Schedule X.

Training of UTM Personnel

- Every UTM Personnel is also obligated to undergo required training as specified under Schedule X of the UAS Rules by an authorized training institute.
- The authorization of such training institute shall be granted by the filing of an application by such institute to the DGCA through the Digital Sky platform in the manner and procedure prescribed under Schedule X of the UAS Rules.
- The validity period for such authorization shall be specified by DGCA and if not, it should be valid for a maximum period of 5 years. For renewal of such license, the applicant shall file an

application in the same manner and procedure prescribed under Schedule X.

- The Training Institute shall also be subjected to inspection and safety oversight by the DGCA at any time.

XVI. Detainment of UAS

- To prevent contravention of UAS Rules- An authority authorized under the Rules shall be authorized to detain a UAS by giving the pilot a written direction or caused any other action which in the opinion of the authority is necessary to make the detention occur including use of force, denial of access to UAS, removal of its parts, etc. Whoever acts in contravention of such direction shall be deemed to be in contravention of the UAS Rules.
- The government officers and the Armed forces can assist the authorized persons in their detention process.

XVII. Laying down of CARs

- The DGCA is authorized to lay down further directions in form Civil Aviation Requirements (CARs) and Circulars in relation to the import, export, sale, manufacturer, use, operation, possession, maintenance, or navigation of UAS operating or registered in India. The only restriction is that they cannot be inconsistent with the Aircraft Act, 1934 and the UAS Draft Rules.
- Before the enactment of such CARs and circulars, the DGCA is required to publish them in their

website for a period of thirty days for inviting suggestions and objections from the public.
- This requirement of publication can be dispensed with by the DGCA for a public interest, the reason for which shall be submitted in writing by them.

XVII. Power of DGCA and the Central Government to exempt

- The DGCA contains the power to exempt any UAS or class of UAS or any individual or class of persons from the application of the CARs issued by them either fully or partially as specified by them in an order which shall be issued by them in writing.
- Similarly, the Central Government contains the power to exempt any UAS or class of UAS or any person or class of persons from the operation of the UAS rules, either fully or partially as specified by them in an order which shall be issued by them in writing.

XVIII. Power to cancel or revoke permissions granted under UAS Rules

- The DGCA or any officer authorized by the Central Government for this purpose contain the power to cancel or suspend any license, certificate, authorization, permit or approval issued to any person under the UAS Rules.
- They can only do so after giving an opportunity of being heard to the concerned person and on being satisfied that there has been a contravention of the UAS rules or any CAR issued by the DGCA in relation to the UAS Rules by the concerned person.

XIX. Inspection

- The DGCA or any officer authorized by them in writing shall have the power to inspect UAS, UAS manufacturing, storage, maintenance facilities or any other facility for the purpose of granting of any authorization, certification or license under the UAS Rules.
- They shall have the authority to carry out surveillance and unannounced inspection of these facilities and shall have the power to inspect, enter and search any premises, documents and interact with any person involved in these facilities and they should be provided complete cooperation by importers, manufacturers, owners, traders and organizations.

XX. Fees

- All fees for permits, licenses, certificates, and other procedures mentioned under UAS Rules, 2020 is prescribed under Schedule XI of the Rules and shall be prescribed in the manner and procedure to be prescribed by the DGCA.

XXI. Penalties

- Any person who contravenes any of the rules mentioned under UAS Rules or directions issued by the DGCA shall be punishable as per the punishment prescribed under the Aircraft Act, 1934 for such contravention and if no such punishment is prescribed, as per the manner prescribed under Schedule XII of the UAS Rules.

- If such contravention occurs due to any accident, the stress of weather or unavoidable cause, then it shall be a defence for the alleged contravener by stating that such contravention took place without his actual fault.
- Additionally, the violation of specific rules under UAS Rules is classified as non-bailable and non-cognizable in nature which is specified under Rule 63.

XXII. Delegation

- Any power conferred on the Central Government under these rules can be exercised by a person authorized by them.
- Any power conferred on the DGCA under these rules can be exercised by a person authorized by the Central Government.

XXIII. Appeal

- Any appeal to any order or decision of the DGCA or Central Authority or any officer authorized by them can be filed to their next higher officer within 60 days of the date of the order, provided not more than two appeals are filed against the same order.

XXIV. Autonomous UAS and Model RPAS

- For these two categories of UAS, the DGCA has stated that such UAS shall operate only in accordance with the specific conditions and defined areas prescribed by them.

- Further, they are automatically exempted from the application of certain rules specified under Rule 53 (1) and Rule 54 (1) of the UAS Rules.
- Additionally, for Autonomous UAS, the DGCA shall also provide conditions and other qualifications of personnel involved in its operation. No such requirement is prescribed for Model RPAS.

V. CHAPTER 7

PROCEDURE:

A. Privacy

- With an estimation of the global increase in usage of drones especially in the commercial sector, a lot of things need to be analyzed. "According to a report by the Federation of Indian Chambers of Commerce and Industry (FICCI) and global consultancy firm, EY, Indian unmanned aerial vehicle (UAV) market is expected to touch $885.7 million by 2021, while the global market size of the drone is pegged at $21.47 billion." With the continuous development of technology, drones are now equipped with various devices such as GPS trackers, high-resolution cameras, facial recognition technologies, etc. and can now be used by drone users to gather unauthorized and personal information and intrusion of private spaces leading to the violation of the rights of individuals. They are also used for surveillance and patrolling by authorities.
- Application of drones in different industries is vast with monitoring, aerial surveillance, imaging which can be linked to AI. With drones having cybersecurity capabilities there are both cons and pros to the industry and the technology.
- Privacy is a concern for the governments, bystanders and other authorities, whose privacy is being breached by the usage of drones. It is for the lawmakers to have a clear path and direction in case of such a breach.

- In India, Right to privacy is a fundamental right under Article 21. The landmark case of *K.S. Puttaswamy v. Union of India* in 2017 bought in the concept of privacy under the broad right to life and personal liberty. Privacy laws are still developing and due to some strong precedents, we have rules in place. Strength to the law is given with every new case, technology, development and many other contributing factors. "Right to Privacy is not only conceded nationally but also internationally under
- various Conventions. Right to Privacy, being a dynamic concept is incorporated under provisions of various legislations and also embraces various aspects.". The judgment overruled M.P Sharma and Kharak Singh. In the latter case, it was ruled that surveillance is necessary to prevent crimes, only in cases of serious encroachment of privacy would there be any violation but not otherwise. K.S. Puttaswamy which now prevails over the two precedents states that any level of violation of privacy will a violation of the law.
- Privacy under the UAS rules 2020 is a compulsory requirement that needs to be addressed at all times by all parties involved in the operation of the drone. However, there is no specific provision made for privacy under the rules. Rule 35 of the draft rules only state that the drones should be flown while protecting the privacy of individuals and property. In such a situation, the privacy bill and the privacy laws of India will apply generally for the drones' industry as they do for others.
- We can expect CARs on privacy for further development for UAVs, however, until then the

rules and the privacy laws in India will be on a developing stage.

- The Draft Rules can also take inspiration from the suggestion provided under previous policies of the Ministry of Civil Aviation. For instance, the draft Drone Policy 2.0 mandates a 'privacy by design' standard. Such criteria would ensure that manufacturers of the drones by design would ensure strict compliance to privacy.

- It is now for the lawmakers and courts to decide on whether a separate CAR would be needed to fill the gap in the draft rules once they are finalized or will the general privacy laws of India cover the needs of the growing technology.

B. <u>Importation and Customs</u>

I. PROCESS FOR IMPORTATION OF DRONES FROM FOREIGN COUNTRIES

- The import procedures under the Draft UAS Rules is a multi- step process where the UAS Importer is firstly required to obtain a Certificate of Manufacture which is required to be obtained by an authorized UAS Manufacturer / UAS Importer to certify that the design of the UAS along with its specification meets the requirements as specified under the Draft UAS Rules.

- One of the conditions for this manufacturer certificate is that entities that intend on importing Drones or their parts or components into India shall have to obtain an Equipment Type Approval (**"ETA"**) from the Wireless Planning and Coordination (**"WPC"**) Wing of India's Department of Telecommunication (**"DoT"**) for operating Drones in de-licensed frequency bands. De-licensed frequency bands are low-frequency bands which facilitate communication between connected vehicles in the automotive industry.

- On obtaining the ETAs, the importers are then required to obtain import clearance from the DGCA. Details of the Drone, including the maximum All-Up-Weight, maximum height attainable, foreign manufacturer details, the purpose of operations and security clearance along with other details are to be provided.
- Based on the import clearance received from the DGCA, the Director-General of Foreign Trade ("DGFT") shall subsequently issue the license for the import of the Drones.
- Additionally, a customs duty equivalent to 28-30% shall be applicable on an imported UAS.
- Only on obtaining the clearance from DGCA and the license from DGFT can the importers then proceed to obtain a unique identification number ("**UIN**") and unmanned aircraft operator permits ("**UAOP**") which are necessary to fly/operate drones in India.

PROCESS FOR LOCALLY MANUFACTURED DRONES

- Under Rule 15 of the new Draft rules, the local manufacturer, as well as foreign manufacturers importing drones, are required to be issued a certificate of manufacturer from the DGCA.
- For the rest of the process for locally manufactured drones, it is quite simple. Once ETA from the WPC wing is granted and the certificate of manufacture is granted, a local manufacturer can simply then approach the DGCA for the issuance of UIN and UAOP. There is no other requirement.

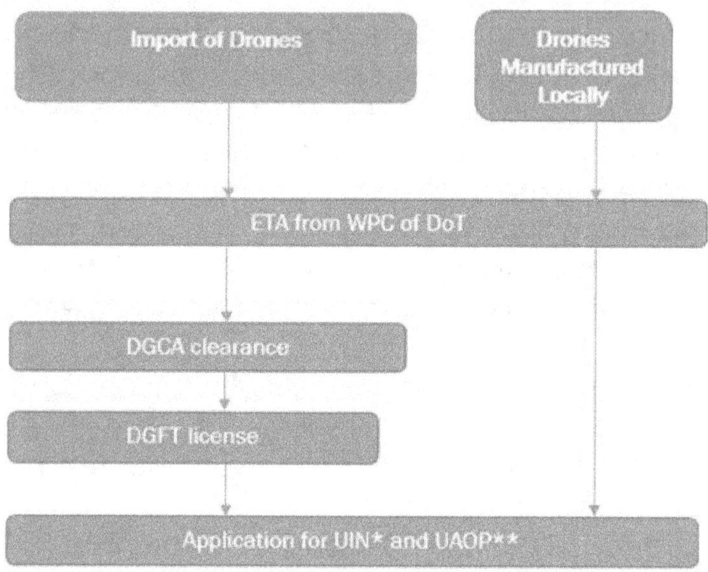

Representation of the importation process for foreign manufactured as well as domestically produced drones in a tabular form.

II. CUSTOMS

Through a notification issued by the Directorate General of Foreign Trade in July 2016, the DGFT declared that the import of Unmanned Aircraft System (UAS)/ Unmanned Aerial Vehicle (UAVs)/ Remotely Piloted Aircraft (RPAs)/ drones are 'Restricted' requiring prior clearance of the Directorate General of Civil Aviation (DGCA) and import license from DGFT. (**DGFT Notification No. 16/2015-2020)**

The above-mentioned policy was recently modified by the Directorate General of Foreign Trade in November 2019 through an issued notification. The DGFT stated that the import of UAS/UAV/RPAS/drones shall remain 'Restricted' and shall require prior clearance of the DGCA and import license from the DGFT. However, for Nano category of drones operating below 50ft/15 meters above ground level, only an ETA approval from the Wiring and Planning Commission (WPC) wing of the Department of Telecommunications shall be required. The requirement for approaching the DGFT and the DGCA before importation was done away with. **(DGFT Notification No. 30/2015-2020)**

Customs authorities have the power to seize these drones/UAVs/UAS/RPAS at ports as per Section 80 of the **Customs Act, 1962**. Goods which are prohibited can be detained. According to section 2(33) of the Customs Act, 1962, "Prohibited goods" means any goods the import or export of which is subject to any prohibition under this Act or any other law for the time being in force. In India, drones are included in the 'restricted' list of items that may be imported in India. Since the importation of drones in violation of statutory provisions have been prohibited in India through the DGFT and the DGCA, the Customs Authorities have a right to regulate its import.

A circular **(F. No. 394/08/2019)** was issued by the Department of Revenue, Ministry of Finance in July, 2019 wherein it was stated that any UAS, RPAS and UAVs of various frequencies bought by the passengers and is being imported by them at any Airports or various ports, in contravention of the Statutory requirements, will be confiscated as per the legal process. The purpose of this circular was to set up guidelines for the manner of such confiscated. The Customs authorities of India approached the Department of Revenue to set up these guidelines.

Also, along with the risk of getting a drone seized, for those individuals who take up the risk of flying drones illegally can end being punished as per **Schedule XII** of the UAS Rules.

III. What Happens to the Seized Drones?

Seized drones are used usually by government authorities.

In September 2019, The Government of India had declared that all drones seized will be handed over to two ministries, Ministry of Home Affairs and Defense Ministry who deal with national security. The ministry shall get all drones free of cost and as per their requirement. **(Circular F. No. 394/08/2019)**

The government had directed that the drones should not be auctioned/sold as such or even in dismantled condition in the open market; and that due to security reasons, these should be handed over to the defence or security forces only.

All the drones of all the categories that will be seized shall be transferred to the warehouses of the following Customs formations, namely, Chennai (Airport), Delhi (IGIA), Kolkata (Airport) and Mumbai (Airport), which shall be the focal Commissionerates for stocking, segregation, a joint inspection by all agencies and distribution.

Handing over of drones will be done after due process and will be distributed equally between the MoD and the MHA (and their constituent organizations/agencies) after a joint inspection that will be conducted by the nodal officers of the MoD and the MHA.

C. FOREIGN COMPANIES' COMMERCIAL USE IN INDIA

Under CAR 1.0

The ongoing Drone Regulations restrict the issue of UINs only to Indian and corporates that are registered and have a principal place of business in India or those where the substantial ownership and effective control is vested in Indian nationals to be eligible to get UINs.

If a foreign citizen or entity wishes to obtain a UIN from the DGCA for commercial purposes, it may do so solely for the purposes of leasing the drone to an Indian citizen or entity or through entering into a partnership with them on a leased basis. They cannot operate it directly under Indian regulations.

Therefore, in order to operate a drone in India, the procurement of a UIN is a mandatory condition and since it is only restricted to Indian nationals and entities under the current regulations, foreign entities can operate their drones only through Indian companies as a mediator.

UAS Draft Rules, 2020

However, under the new draft rules, the lease criteria have been removed and the process for foreign entities has become more stringent. An owner/operator can now only lease their drones to an *authorized person* under the Draft Rules.

According to these rules, every individual or corporate body dealing with UAS in any capacity in India shall be authorized by the DGCA to do so. This requirement applies for owners, operators, manufacturers, traders as well as importers according to Rule 5 of the Draft UAS Rules.

But this authorization is only restricted to Indian entities and individuals. Foreign companies can be allowed if, they meet the below-mentioned criteria,

Rule 7 of the UAS Rule states that,

Eligibility Conditions for Authorisation. — A person referred in rule 5 may be granted authorisation subject to fulfilment of following eligibility conditions—

(i) an individual who is
a) a citizen of India,
b) and (b) 18 years of age or more; or

(ii) a company or a body corporate provided that
a) it is registered and has its principal place of business within India, and
b) the Chairman and at least two-thirds of its directors are citizens of India;

(iii) a firm or an association of persons or body of individuals or a local authority or any legal entity, whether incorporated or not, Central and State Government or an agency thereof:

Provided that for clauses (ii) and (iii) of this rule, the substantial ownership and effective control shall vest in Indian nationals.

Therefore, since foreign entities and individuals are quite restricted from being registered as an Authorized Person under the rules, they are restricted in the Indian market to a large extent. Considering their capabilities and potential, not allowing foreign entities and individuals to operate and own drones in India causes hindrance to the growth of the drone industry along with disincentivising foreign investments in India by foreign players.

D. <u>Pilot Training</u>

- The current law governing Pilot Training of Remote Pilots is the CAR, Series X, Part 1, Section 3 on Air Transport. Paragraph 9 talks about the requirement of training of the pilot, to be obtained through a DGCA approved Flying Training Organisation (FTO).
- There's no mention on continuous training in the UAS draft rules, which might be required in situations where there's a gap in flying or when the pilot suffers from a serious medical issue. (Rule 33 and Schedule VII)
- There are two types of pilot: Qualified and licensed pilot. A 'Qualified Remote Pilot' needs to undergo the required training imparted by an authorized training organization as per procedure under Schedule VII. The DGCA shall issue the UAS pilot license as per procedure in Schedule VII. Flying a Nano drone requires no training as per the draft rules.
- Air Traffic Management Service- The Draft UAS Rules establish a UTM set-up wherein the air traffic is managed by personnel who have obtained the required training and license to engage in

providing air traffic management services. Persons must obtain training as imparted by an authorized training organization.

- Since the draft rules have made training mandatory for pilots, many pilot training organisations and institutions have emerged. They are governed by CARs issued by the DGCA.
- "Under the draft, the entities that can apply to become RPTOs are:
a. Central or state government or their undertaking or autonomous Bodies,
b. Government-approved universities,
c. DGCA approved FTOs, NSOPs, SOPs, Domestic CAR-147 approved Maintenance Training Organisations, CAR-145 approved CAMOs and CAR 21 approved Design Organisations,
d. Remotely Piloted Aircraft manufacturers"
- Anyone who is interested in starting a Remote Pilot Training Organization (RPTO) will have to obtain a NOC which will be valid for up to two years.
- "To apply for a NOC, an applicant will have to submit evidence of having funds of at least Rs 10 lakh in the form of paid-up capital, project report containing details of the proposed set-up including 3 years' business plan, proposed financial structure, ownership pattern, time frame for operationalization of the project, RPA types to be used and its suitability for flying training, human resource, and maintenance support, among other things."
- DGCA has also mandated some infrastructural requirements that have to be followed by the applicants while establishing the institutions. Once all the steps are satisfied with, DGCA gives

approval for five years which is extendable by 5 more years on fulfilling all the requirements above.

- As per the draft rules, an inspection of such institutions can take place at any reasonable time.

Procedure and rules for training of an observer:

- Besides training of the operator, as also mentioned in the rules, it is important that the observers, launch crew and recovery crew all have their set of training as well.
- As the rules prohibit drones from flying BVLOS, an observer is needed at all times to have an eye on the drone.
- The general responsibility of an observer can be to access the flying conditions for clear airspace.
- An observer should not only be able to identify issues in the sky but also direct the operator to take necessary actions.
- It is important for the observer to remember at all times that the instruction being passed down to the operator should be according to the operator's position and not the observers.
- Both operator and observer should be close enough to communicate with one another without being an interference.
- Emergency procedures and alternate landing locations shall be discussed well in advance.
- During the training of the observer, certain keywords and phrases should be taught so that there is easy and uniformity in communication.
- For the training of the staff and crew involved in the maintenance of the UAS, the Draft UAS rules (under Rule 16) prescribe certain provisions.

- Firstly, every importer or manufacturer of UAS is obligated to provide a maintenance manual to traders, owners and operators of UAS as part of their mandatory sale documents.
- This manual shall consist of information regarding maintenance requirements of UAS to operate in India. The manufacturer or importer is also obligated to provide training to the personnel, staff and crew involved in the maintenance of UAS in accordance with the requirements mentioned in the manual.
- They can also set up maintenance centres that shall consist of trained personnel that shall carry out maintenance procedures for the UAS of their respective customers including traders, owners and operators.
- India lacks infrastructure and regulation in this area but is moving towards its development. Recently, in August 2020, the Bureau of Civil Aviation Security (BCAS) issued guidelines for drone operating systems. One of the guidelines stated that background check of not only the remote pilots operating UAS shall be carried out but also of visual observers, launch crew and recovery crew involved in the operation of UAS. The authorities are recognizing their contribution.

Following is the list of drone pilot training schools approved by the DGCA:

1. **<u>Bombay Flying Club</u>**- It is based in Maharashtra and is a private institution. It is the first DGCA approved drone training school in India. The School offers the following courses- Ground Training, Simulator training, one on

one practical flying, solo flying, instrument flying and exposure to various emergency procedure.

2. **Flytech**- It is based in Telangana and is a private training institution. It offers the following courses- Student Pilot License, Private Pilot License and Commercial Pilot License.

3. **GATI** – It is based in Odisha and is a government training institution. The school offers the following courses- Night Rating, Instrument Rating, Frtol, Hobby Flying and Multi Training.

4. **Telangana State Aviation Academy (TSAA)**- It is based in Telangana and is the second government Drone training institution. It also offers the above-mentioned courses.

E. **Insurance**

Draft Rules, 2020 – *"52. Insurance of UAS. — (1) No UA shall be operated in India unless there is in existence a valid third party insurance policy to cover the liability that may arise on account of a mishap involving such UA and causing death or bodily injury to any person or damage to property. (2) The compensation payable in such cases shall be assessed in such a manner and procedure as specified in the Motor Vehicles Act, 1988 and rules made thereunder."*

India based HDFC ERGO is partnering with TropoGo, a startup, for launching pay as you fly, insurance policy for drone owners in India. It will cover the third-party liabilities claims for property or bodily injury. It will cover commercial drone owners and operators. A committee has been set up by IRDAI to suggest insurance procedures for drones (June 2020).

UAS being a new industry in India, there are no insurance policies that exist for the parties involved. However, the USA and UK having established industries can be used as examples for the insurance policies in India.

Companies in India recognise the need for such policies as the market is growing. Especially after Covid-19, and the introduction of draft rules, there has been an expansion on how drones are seen in India. At the same time, one recognises the damage and breach that a drone can cause.

India lacks the infrastructure to support insurance policies for drones. Companies also do not have standards set or rules which can be the basis for the insurance policies. The lack of cases and experience with the drone industry makes the process of developing insurance policies difficult.

Insurance companies can take examples from the USA and UK. Companies in the USA provide insurance for payload, ground equipment and even privacy breach. Another solution can be a detailed provision for insurance under the rules so that the companies know what needs to be covered under different policies and who needs to get these insurances. The rules can also have the minimum amount of insurance to be taken so that there is uniformity among the authorised personnel. UK, Germany and France also have insurances for drones that cover public liability.

Two types of drone insurance offered:

- <u>Drone liability insurance</u> – is an aviation liability insurance, covers the cost of damage caused to another person due to technical defect or error

- <u>Drone hull insurance -</u> covers up your expenses, in situations, where your drone breaks or gets damaged while operating, this insurance will cover the cost of repairs or a new purchase.

There are seven things that must be kept in mind while completing your insurance requirements:

o Intended use
o Coverage
o Number of drone users
o Number of copters
o Flight areas

o Scope of Drone insurance and
o Price

F. <u>Beyond Visual Line of Operations (BVLOS)</u>

- The CAR issued on 1st December 2018, also known as CAR 1.0 currently governs the drones operated in India. It does not mention the BVLOS operations in its document.
- The new UAS draft rules 2020 also, only mention the definition of BVLOS under Rule 2(10), as an operation of drone which happens beyond the visual sight of the remote pilot and the observer. But, even the Rules fail to mention anything more than that on this topic.
- The Draft CAR 2.0, introduced in pursuance of CAR 1.0, gives recommendations of expansion of drones to be operated as BVLOS and above the current height of 400 feet.
- However, this type of technology is largely used to operate military drones and is still being put to test by companies for commercial usage.

- BVLOS requires a long-range Telemetry to be on a UAV which enables it to transmit data such as the altitude, speed and position and other necessary parameters required to control an aircraft.
- These types of operations can be conducted through an RPAS or through an autonomous aircraft, but because unlike the drone operated within the visual sight, these pilots operating these type of flights need additional training.
- On 13th May 2019, DGCA issued an invitation to the drone industrial players for an Expression of Interest (EOI) who wish to conduct experimental BVLOS operations of RPAS in India, for at least two months to collect evidence and then submit proof of concept (POC) to the DGCA.
- These experiments are only allowed to be conducted in controlled conditions within identified and segregated low altitude airspaces across the country that have been identified by the DGCA and the AAI.
- This creates an evidence-based regulatory framework, enabling a potential change/ growth of the drone industry.
- From delivery of consumer products to delivery of medical supplies to surveillance of traffic, construction sites etc., companies from all spheres applied to conduct such experimental operations under the supervision of the DGCA for development of new regulations for this growing industry.
- The abovementioned invitation-only allowed such experiments to be conducted by a Consortium, meaning a team of expert agencies and service providers. Each one of such consortium must consist of:-

- □ *Project Coordinator* – Will represent the consortium and act as a single point of contact
- □ *UAS Operator* – Responsible for operations of drones, and ensuring compliance with all safety standards
- □ *UTM service provider* - Will provide services of UAS Traffic Management and coordinate with the ATC
- □ *Supplementary service provider* - Provide 3D maps, weather data, surveillance data etc.
- □ *Agencies for data acquisition & Analysis* - Collect, collate and analyze data
- □ *SMS Expert* - Responsible for preparation of safety case and Proof of Concept (POC).
- A minimum of 100 hours of experimental BVLOS flight must be completed by each consortium before preparing a POC and submitting it to the DGCA for approval.
- Each proposal submitted to the DGCA will be evaluated by the BVLOS Experiment Assessment and Monitoring (BEAM) committee, constituted by MoCA, which might accept or reject or demand amendments to the proposal.
- As of June 2020, the DGCA has granted permission to around 10 consortia for conducting such experiments.
- DGCA has approved consortia of Dunzo Digital, a hyperlocal startup, which has partnered with Alternative Global India, a management consulting firm, to enable Drone delivery flights in India. They are planning to have 100 hours of BVLOS trials in order to learn and adapt to the best available technologies. This consortium has a total of 8 members who are contributing to various their expertise in various fields like UTM, UAV system, LTE, 3D mapping etc.

- Another consortium led by ANRA technologies will focus on the delivery of medical supplies, including blood and medicines and it has also partnered up with Swiggy, India's biggest food delivery platforms for enabling contactless delivery of food. This ANRA-led consortium includes Swiggy; Indian Institute of Technology, Ropar; and BetterDrones, an Indian drone service provider providing a network of trained pilots.
- Another partnership between Altitude Angel, a U.K based UTM technology provider and Sagar Defence Engineering Ltd., based in Mumbai, is seeking to enable BVLOS operations for a multitude of services like medical and cargo delivery, surveillance operations, search and rescue and survey and mapping.
- All these consortium/ partnerships formed between companies are in their trial phase as of now, and we can soon expect them to be functioning after submission of their proof of concept to the DGCA and subsequent approval.

G. Permissions required from ATC, MoCA, MoD, WPC, DGFT, DGCA, HOME AFFAIRS UNDER UAS RULES, 2020

Permissions required from the DGCA

- Under the UAS Rules, 2020, all persons associated with the drone industry in India shall get authorized by the DGCA including importers, manufacturers, Traders, owners, operators to act in their particular

- capacities in India. They can be authorized by applying to the DGCA through the digital sky platform in accordance to the manner and procedure prescribed under Schedule I, after which they will be granted a **Unique Authorization Number (UAN)** to act as an authorized person.
- An authorized importer shall procure an **import clearance** by making an application in the manner and procedure prescribed under Schedule II of the UAS Rules to the DGCA before importing a UAS in India.
- For authorized importers and manufacturers of UAS and its parts and components, a **'Certificate of Manufacturer'** is to be procured from the DGCA which certifies that their design is in compliance to the requirements under UAS Rules specified under Schedule II. The application shall be made to the DGCA in the manner and procedure prescribed under Schedule II.
- One of the requirements for this Certificate of Manufacture under Schedule II is **NPNT compliance.** As per the No Permission No Take-off rule, the drone shall be fixed with the NPNT compliant devices, only after which the DGCA will approve the said drone. The requirement has to fulfilled by the manufacturer so that the drone can be certified, inspected and approved for use.
- The DGCA shall also be responsible for appointing **testing laboratories and organizations** that shall be responsible for ensuring that the products of authorized importers and manufacturers are in compliance with the manufacturing requirements specified under Schedule II.

- The owner, traders, and operators on the receiving end of **maintenance manuals** being provided by manufacturers and importers shall ensure that their UAS is being maintained in accordance with the manuals and shall maintain a record of such maintenance to the DGCA.
- For a UAS to be operated or owned in India, they shall be allotted a **Unique Identification Number (UIN)** by the DGCA. An authorized manufacturer or importer shall make an application to the DGCA as per the manner and procedure prescribed under Schedule III.
- A registered owner of a UAS is obligated to notify to the DGCA in the manner prescribed by them in case of any **transfer of ownership** by him, if a **UAS ceases to be owned** by him if the **UAS is damaged or beyond repair** and if there has been a **loss of UAS** or it has been announced missing. On being satisfied with the presence of any of these conditions, the DGCA deregisters the UAS.
- A **non-compliant UAS** imported or manufactured in India on or before the date specified by the Central Government (the date of enactment of the Draft UAS Rules) can be accepted by the DGCA in the manner and procedure prescribed under Schedule V.
- Every **UAS operator** (except for the nano category) shall procure a permit in the manner and procedure prescribed under Schedule VI of the UAS rules by the DGCA. The operating conditions of the UAS shall be prescribed by the DGCA in the permit issued by them.
- For operations of UAS, other than Nano and Micro category of UAS, a **Qualified Remote Pilot** license is required for the one operating the UAS. The

DGCA shall grant this license as per the manner and procedure prescribed under Schedule VII of the Draft Rules.

- One of the requirements for being a Qualified Remote Pilot is that they shall undergo training from an **authorized training institute** as per the manner prescribed under Schedule VII. The DGCA shall be the one granting authorization to such institutes. They shall file an application to them in the manner and procedure prescribed under Schedule VII.
- **Permission to fly-** No UAS shall operate in India unless permission has been granted by the DGCA through the Digital Sky platform in the manner and procedure prescribed by the DGCA.
- UAS regulation in India prohibits the **carriage of payload** by any UAS, except as permitted by the DGCA.
- The **dropping of any articles** from a UAS in motion is prohibited in India, except in the manner and procedure specified by the DGCA.
- All UAS operators are obliged to comply with the **Rules of Air** that shall be issued by the DGCA in pursuance to the enactment of the UAS Rules.
- A person seeking to set up a **drone port** for the purpose such as arrival, departure, movements and other activities associated to UAS, shall make an application in the manner and procedure prescribed under Schedule IX of the UAS Rules to the DGCA through the Digital Sky Platform for obtaining authorization or a license for drone port.
- A person intending to provide UTM Services shall file an application to the DGCA in the manner and procedure prescribed under Schedule X of the UAS Rules to get a **UTM License.**

- Any person who shall engage in UTM Services in the Indian Airspace or Foreign Airspace (under any International arrangement) shall also procure a **UTM personnel license** by filing an application to the DGCA in the manner and procedure prescribed under Schedule X of the UAS Rules.
- Every UTM Personnel is obligated to undergo required training as specified under Schedule X of the UAS Rules by an authorized training institute. The **authorization of such training institute** shall be granted by the filing of an application by such institute to the DGCA through the Digital Sky platform in the manner and procedure prescribed under Schedule X of the UAS Rules.

Permissions required from the DGFT

- For importation, after the application under Schedule II is submitted to the DGCA for import clearance, they transfer it to the DGFT who determines whether such clearance shall be issued or not. The DGT issues such clearance based on their own norms.

Permissions required from the WPC

- One of the pre-requisites for this Certificate of Manufacture is that the applicant shall first procure an **'equipment type approval' (ETA)** from the
Wireless Planning and Coordination (WPC) wing of the Department of Telecommunications. This is an approval granted to allow the operation of drones in de-licensed frequency bands as well as for details of emergency recovery systems. This requirement exists for both, locally manufactured as well as imported drones.

Permissions required from the Ministry of Home Affairs

- For foreign pilots, a security clearance shall be issued by the Ministry of Home Affairs in addition to them having a Remote Pilot's License which is granted by the DGCA.
- For getting authorized by the DGCA through the Issuance of a Unique Identification Number, one of the requirements under Schedule I of the UAS Rules is that security clearance shall be needed from the Ministry of Home Affairs (MHA) for UAS importers/ traders/ manufacturers having their principal place of business in a country other than India.
- Also, one of the non-operation areas specified under Schedule VIII of the UAS Rules, specifies that no UAS shall be permitted to operate within 2 kilometers from the perimeter of strategic locations/ vital installations notified by the Ministry of Home Affairs unless clearance is obtained from MHA.

Permission required from the Ministry of Environment, Forests and Climate Change

- One of the non-operation areas specified under Schedule VIII of the UAS Rules, specifies that no UAS shall be permitted to operate over eco-sensitive zones around National Parks and Wildlife Sanctuaries notified by the Ministry of Environment, Forests and Climate Change without prior permission from them.

Permissions required from the ATC

- Currently, all drone operators intending to operate in controlled airspace are required to establish and maintain contact with the nearest ATC unit. ATC services for drones are provided by the Airports Authority of India.
- However, under the Draft Rules, 2020, the Central Government has been authorized to establish an Unmanned Aircraft Traffic Management System in the Indian Airspace specifically for UAS operation and the UAS Rules prescribe specific provisions dealing with it.

<u>Permissions required from the Ministry of Defense</u>

- Before the declaration of areas into red and yellow zones for UAS operations, the approval of the Ministry of Defense is required by the DGCA.

<u>Roles and Responsibilities of Various Government Authorities under the current drone regulations</u>

Director General of Civil Aviation

- Import Clearance
- Issuance of UIN
- Issuance of UAOP
- Renewal of UAOP
- Suspension/Cancellation of UIN & UAOP, if one violates or failes to comply with the regulation

Director General of Foriegn Trade

- Import Licence

Ministry of Home Affairs

- Security Clearance

Ministry of Defence

- Permission for following activities over the restricted/prohibited areas on case-tocase basis
- Aerial survey
- Imageries
- Videography
- Still photography

Indian Air Force

- Air Defece Clearance
- Monitoring movement of RPA in the country

Wireless Planning and Coordination Wing, DOT

- Equipment Type Approval (ETA) or License for RPA

Bureau of Civil Aviation Security

- Security Programme Approval

Airport Authority of India

- Approval of Flight Plan
- Monitoring Movement of RPA in the country

Local Police Authority

- Enforcement of violators as per applicable IPCs

H. Flying Zones and Conditions

Flying zones

The Digital Sky platform has categorized the Indian airspace into a different zone; Red, Yellow, and Green.

The Red Zone is known as the "no-fly zone", no Remote Pilot Aircraft is allowed to operate in this area specified. Para 13 of CAR 1.0 specifies such area where no RPA shall be flown;

a) Within a distance of 5 km from the perimeter of airports at Mumbai, Delhi, Chennai, Kolkata, Bengaluru, and Hyderabad;

b) Within a distance of 3 km from the perimeter of any civil, private or defence airports, other than those mentioned in Para 13.1(a);

c) Above the Obstacle Limitation Surfaces (OLS) or PANS-OPS surfaces, whichever is lower, of an operational aerodrome, specified in Ministry of Civil Aviation (Height Restrictions for Safeguarding of Aircraft Operations) Rules, 2015 notified through Gazette of India notification GSR751(E) as amended from time to time;

d) Within permanent or temporary Prohibited, Restricted and Danger Areas including TRA, and TSA, as notified in AIP;

e) Within 25km from the international border which includes Line of Control (LoC), Line of Actual Control (LAC) and Actual Ground Position Line (AGPL);

f) Beyond 500 m (horizontal) into the sea from coastline provided the location of the ground station is on a fixed platform over land;

g) Within 3 km from the perimeter of military installations/ facilities/ where military activities/ exercises are being carried out unless clearance is obtained from the local military installation/facility;

h) Within a 5 km radius from Vijay Chowk in Delhi. However, this is subject to any additional conditions/ restrictions imposed by local law enforcement agencies/ authorities because of the security.

i) Within 2 km from the perimeter of strategic locations/ vital installations notified by Ministry of Home Affairs unless clearance is obtained from MHA;

j) Within 3 km from the radius of State Secretariat Complex in State Capitals;

k) From a mobile platform such as a moving vehicle, ship or aircraft;

l) Over eco-sensitive zones around National Parks and Wildlife Sanctuaries notified by the Ministry of Environment, Forests and Climate Change without prior permission.

Under the UAS draft rule, 2020, Rule 34 mentions, the "no operational area" to be the area where a person shall not fly or assist in flying an Unmanned Aircraft at any times. Under the draft rules, the no-operation areas are specified under Schedule VIII. Along with this, No RPA shall carry out aerial photography/remote sensing surveys over the areas specified in Para 13.1 of this CAR. (similar provision under Rule 35 of UAS Draft Rules,2020). In case one requires to operate within such a zone, DGCA may authorize it on case to case basis subject to the approval of the Ministry of Defense. In such a case, the application shall be submitted to Director Regulations & Information, DGCA (seven copies) in the prescribed format as indicated at Annexure-XI of CARs 1.0.

<u>The Yellow Zone</u> is the controlled area means an airspace of defined dimensions within which air traffic control service is provided in accordance

with the airspace classification. To operate in such area one is required to obtain an Air Defense Clearance/ Flight Information Centre (FIC) number from the ATC. The Map of the yellow zone is yet to be approved by the Ministry of Defense. Once the approval is given, Yellow zones will become active.

<u>The Green Zones</u> are the uncontrolled areas or the unrestricted areas where the ATC services are not provided. The operator needs to obtain clearance from the digital sky platform to be NPNT compliant to facilitate operation in this zone. The Ministry of Civil Aviation through its order dated 03 April 2020 has approved six green zone sites.

The sites are geometric circles, each with 10 km radius (area 78.5 sq km each) with their center points located at:

1) 1. 15°30'15.5"N 78°29'29.5"E (Nandyal, Andhra Pradesh)

2) 2. 13°39'56.1"N 77°20'36.2"E (Tumkur, Karnataka)

3) 3. 18°18'18.0"N 73°11'19.0"E (Sonsade, Maharashtra)

4) 4. 27°59'26.8"N 76°23'04.2"E (Neemrana, Rajasthan)

5) 5. 12°42'55.0"N 79°16'45.9"E (Arani, Tamilnadu)

6) 6. 22°41'49.5"N 87°35'03.5"E (Kharsa, West Bengal)

Drone flights in the Six green zones sites will need to be compliant with the applicable conditions of DGCA CARs 1.0.

Flying Conditions

As per Para 12 of CARs 1.0, the following requirements of flying an RPA need to be followed.

a) All RPA shall operate within the visual line of sight and restricted to fly during the day time only.
b) RPA operations except those in enclosed premises, shall be conducted only when the following meteorological conditions exist:
1. During daylight (between sunrise and sunset).
2. In Visual Meteorological Conditions (VMC) with minimum ground visibility of 5 km and cloud ceiling not less than 1500 feet (450 m).
3. Surface winds of not more than 10 knots or as specified by the manufacturer.
4. No precipitation (rain, hail, or snow) or thunderstorm activities, or exceeding those specified by the manufacturer.

c) The operator [except Nano intending to operate up to 50 ft (15 m) AGL in uncontrolled airspace/ enclosed premises] shall obtain permission before undertaking flight through 'Digital Sky Platform'

Operation of RPA beyond the conditions specified on point (a) and (b) as mentioned above may be authorized by DGCA on case to case basis if there is adequate justification provided by the applicant for the safe conduct of RPAS operations.

VI. CHAPTER 8

WAY FORWARD

On 16th July 2020, the Ministry of Civil Aviation at a press conference addressed the challenges present in the current regulatory system for drones. The introduced the actions taken by them for dealing with these challenges and to ensure the development of the drone industry.

A. Challenges

They started by addressing the present challenges that included,

1. Drone technology is evolving faster than the policy and regulatory regime
2. Significant concerns around national security, criminal acts, safety, and privacy violations
3. Artificially suppressed demand for drone services in India
4. Huge dependence on imported drone components
5. Inadequate funding and insurance for startups
6. Negligible budget for drone research and development

B. Government initiatives

Actions undertaken by the Drone regulatory body to overcome these challenges was also introduced at this conference. Some of them include,

- Draft CAR for drone training released for public feedback on 14 Jun 2020
- Discussions on for DISHA Fund for research and development (Drones for infrastructure, security, healthcare, and agriculture).
- DISHA FUND- The Ministry of Civil Aviation is working towards funding the research and development of unmanned aircraft. Funds will provide financial support to small and medium enterprises so they can manufacture UAVs in four sectors- infrastructure, security, healthcare, and agriculture. DISHA is referred to as Drone Innovation for Security Healthcare and Agriculture.
- UAS Traffic Management (UTM) policy being drafted
- Efforts on to streamline certification of drones through Quality Council of India (QCI) and renowned Qualification Bodies (QB)-who will draft SOPs to qualify drones
- Discussions on with security agencies for counter-drone solutions
- Regular interaction carried out with Indian drone entrepreneurs to understand their challenges and to take corrective actions thereof
- Fast track approvals given to Ministry of Agriculture, Survey of India, Maharashtra Transco, Indian Oil, state govt for drone operations and more approvals being considered
- Digital sky platform phase I going live on 2nd October 2020 to bring modification to the platform in pursuance to the new rules:

a. Modification of Digital Sky Platform as per UAS Rules 2020.
b. Online Integration with other government entities.

c. Airspace management workflows.
d. Flight Plan Approval.
e. Post-Flight data submission
f. Reports and dashboards.

All green zones are activated on the digital sky platform. Red and yellow still to be activated waiting for approval by MoD

i. The designated six green zone sites were approved on 3 April 2020.
ii. The sites were circles with 5km radius (area 78.5 sq km each) with their Centre points at
  1. 15°30'15.5" N 78°29'29.5" E (Nandyal, Andhra Pradesh)
  2. 13°39'56.1"N 77°20'36.2'E (Tumkar, Karnataka)
  3. 18°18'18.0"N 73°11'19.0"E (Sonsade, Maharashtra)
  4. 27°59'26.8"N 76°23'04.2"E (Neemrana, Rajasthan)
  5. 12°42'55.0"N 79°16'45.9"E (Arani, Tamil Nadu)
  6. 22°41'49.5"N 87°35'03.5"E (Kharsa, West Bengal)

- All flights in the green areas have been activated on 4th July 2020.

- Government projects where DGCA granted approvals:

1. <u>An Outline of Anti Locust Operations:</u>

- 20th May: Request for Aerial Spraying received from Agriculture Ministry.

- 21st May: MoCA provides fast track approval with due safeguards.

- 27th May: Inter-ministerial Empowered Committee (EC) formed.

- 01 June: EC Concludes negotiations with drone companies.

- 03 June: EC submits the report to the agriculture ministry

- 06 June: Work orders issued to five drone companies.

- 09 June: Drone warriors reach Rajasthan.

2. <u>SVAMITVA</u> – Aerial mapping of villages

- The survey of India has been given fast track approval by the DGCA to map villages in India using drones to ensure accurate land records, financial benefits for owners and dispute resolution
- SVAMITVA stands for - "Survey of Villages and Mapping with improvised technology in village areas".
- Immediate Target is to map approximately 1 lakh Villages by December 2020.
- By December 2024, it will fulfill the long term target to map India's 6.6 Lakh Villages.
- This will entail the creation of more jobs for the unemployed and local production of drones.

3. <u>Power-line inspections in Maharashtra</u>

- Maharashtra Transco has been approved by DGCA to inspect the powerline using drones. Inspections through drones enable cheaper and more efficient results
- Drones enhance the quality of inspection at a fraction of the cost and human risk.
- Many other similar utilities are likely to get approvals closer to the date.
- Many large opportunities have opened for young drones' entrepreneurs.

4. Oil pipeline inspection

- Indian Oil has been approved by the DGCA to inspect pipelines using drones. This prevents oil theft and unauthorized usage.
- There will be an enhanced quality of inspection that has never been seen before at such a small fraction of a cost.
- There will be a multitude of loss eliminations and prevent corruption.
- Many private oil companies will get approvals sooner.

5. Drone Training

- DGCA approved flying schools were authorized by DGCA to provide drone training. A Draft CAR was released on 14th June 2020 for drone training.
- IGRUA (Amethi, UP) has shown keen interest in Drone Training Schools.
- There will be many Drone schools training that has already been proposed and given that right to provide that education to numerous entities such as:

i.   All Government and Autonomous Bodies,
ii.   Government-approved universities,
iii.   DGCA- approved drone manufacturers
iv.   DGCA- approved FTOs, NSOPs, SOPs, domestic entities approved under CAR-147, CAR-145, and CAR 21.

Suggested Proposals:

- There should be continuous reforms in drone policies and regulations.
- Provide fast track approvals for mass benefit use cases, especially in infrastructure, agriculture, healthcare, defense, and national security.
- Build support for the proposed DISHA fund (DISHA- 'Drones for infrastructure, security, healthcare, and agriculture')
- Engage closely with academicians, young entrepreneurs, and industry to further develop drone technology in India.
- Push immensely for "Make in India, Make for the World" under the Atmanirbhar Bharat.

C.   Forecast of Drone Market Report

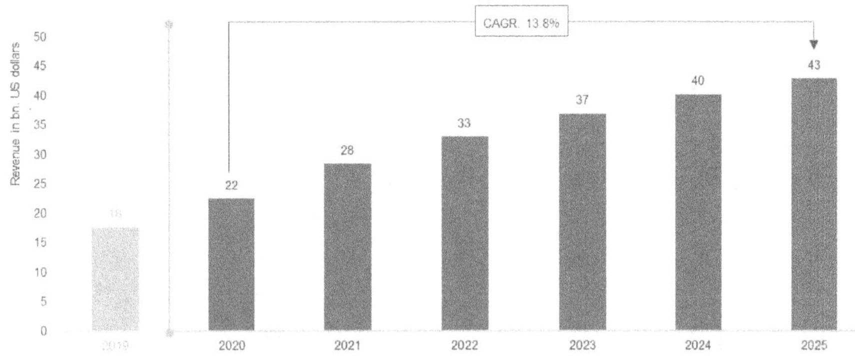

Source: Drone Industry Insights; Drone Market Report 2020;
June/2020

Drone Market Size & Forecast per Region

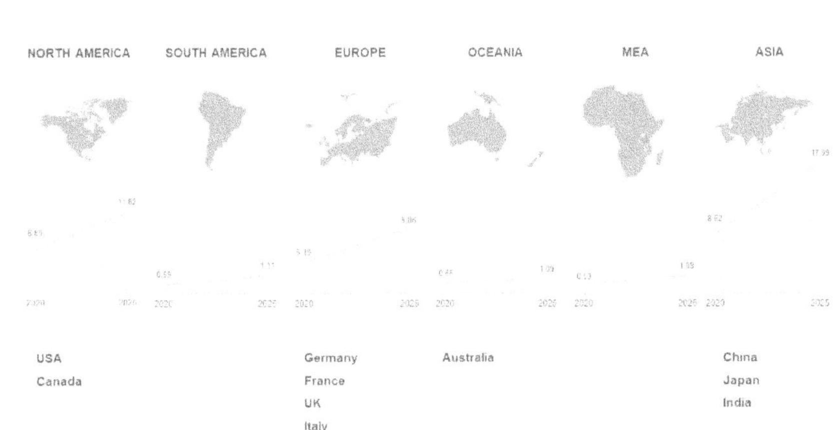

Source: Drone Industry Insights; Drone Market Report 2020;
June/2020

VII.   CHAPTER 9

FAQs

1. When will the digital sky platform begin to operate? The platform has been in plans since the 2018 1.0 policy, however the same still has not been put into operation.

- The Digital sky platform is since its beginning, in a beta phase, and simply is accepting applications such as Unique Identification Number and Unmanned Aircraft Operator Permits.

- A lot of mechanisms such as taking permission from the authorities before the flight of aircraft systems are missing. There is no clarity provided by DGCA as to when such a system will be developed and be fully operational.

- It is advisable to have an alternate paper-based approach for authorization being provided by the DGCA until the platform is fully operational.

2. What changes have been made from the previous drafts?

- The Draft Rules, 2020 are by and large like the existing CAR 1.0 with some notable changes.

- It introduces the extra-territorial application of these rules to every UAS registered in India.

- new definitions such as BVLOS, Drone Port, Drone Corridors, UAS Traffic Management have been added.

- procedural requirements such as getting an import clearance for 'parts and components' whereas earlier an import clearance was required only for the entire UAS.

- Certificate for a Manufacturer of UAS is also added under the rules.
- relaxations are granted to micro and nano drones from procedural compliances.
- DGCA has been given wider powers like, right to inspect, maintain safety, and to detain drones and manufacturers and new criminal provisions have also been added. Certain defenses can also be claimed by the accused.
- All the gaps in the proper implementation of the rules will be filled later by the implementation of detailed CARs by the DGCA.

3. What is the procedure to make new CARs in pursuance to new Draft Rules 2020?

- Under rule 56 of the UAS Rules, the DGCA has the power to issue directions through the Publication of CARs or circulars concerning the import, export, manufacture, sale, use, operation, possession, maintenance, or navigation of UAS operating or registered in India.
- The only restriction is that the DGCA cannot release orders that are inconsistent with the Aircraft Act, 1937, or the UAS Rules, 2020 in any way.

4. Will the CARs to the rules also be open to questions and challenges to the public like the UAS Rules 2020?

- Under Rule 56 of the UAS Rules, 2020, if the DGCA exercises their power of publishing new CARs or orders, they shall place it on their website for 30 days for inviting suggestions and objections from the public.

- However, the DGCA also has the right to dispense with the requirement of inviting such objections or suggestions for 30 days. They can only do so for public interest and shall give such order in writing.

5. Do the UAS rules 2020 comply with international standards?

- In 2015, the International Civil Aviation released a Manual on Remotely Piloted Aircraft Systems to provide guidelines to various contracting states in drafting their Drone policies. It highlighted various issues such as regulatory issues, legal matter, certification of aircraft and systems, licensing, etc. India too, referred to this manual while drafting its policy. But they could make changes accordingly because the Manual was devised just to provide guidance.

- As per binding international standards, there does not exist one yet that all countries must adhere to. The International Organization for Standardization only recently in 2019, published the first International Standard for UAS and specifies internationally agreed and accepted requirements for safe commercial operations since there is variation in drone laws of all countries. (ISO 21384-3:2019). But adherence to these standards depends on the will of the country. India has not chosen to adopt such standards as of now.

6. What is the legal usage of Drones?

Drones, also known as Unmanned Aircraft Systems, are used for various civilian, commercial, governmental, and military purposes in India. Because of the developing technology and the popularity drones are gaining in today's world, their usage is becoming endless. It includes monitoring, inspection, surveillance, mapping, delivery, rescue, and search operations.

7. Is there a problem with privacy and security in using a technology of such a nature?

- As Unmanned Aircraft systems become less expensive and more accessible, there is an increasing threat of invasion of privacy of individuals and property with their increased usage. Additionally, with the development of new technology, new threats are emerging such as unauthorized data acquisition and breach of data.
- Under CAR 1.0 and UAS Draft Rules, 2020, both, privacy compliance is mentioned specifically. However, the former states that compliance with the 'privacy norms of an entity' shall be ensured. There is no explanation provided on what such norms will be. Therefore, there was a lot of criticism received on the lack of clarity and the levy of penalties on violations.
- The Draft rules, 2020 move a step further and tries to bring some clarity into the privacy question. It specifies that the 'privacy of a person and property' shall be ensured during the operation of UAS.

8. Will there be a distinction between military usage and commercial/ civil usage?

The UAS Draft Rules, 2020 was drafted to regulate civil and commercial UAS. However, no distinction is made in the text of the rules between UAS used for commercial/civil use and those used for

Military use. There is a false perception created that these rules apply to both types of UAS. Therefore, there is a need to mention a distinction.

9. What will be the procedures and consequences in cases of accidents? Will it depend on the intensity of the same?

- Under the Draft Rules, 2020, the Registered owner of the UAS shall notify the DGCA if their UAS is damaged beyond repair or there is a loss of their UAS. The DGCA then can deregister the UIN of the UA if they are satisfied that the UA is destroyed, permanently withdrawn from use, is missing, or is non-traceable. Additionally, they are also required to notify the DGCA if there is any change of ownership of the UAS.

- CAR 1.0 mentioned the term 'accident' also in the list of things to be reported however, this term has been omitted from the Draft Rules, 2020. In terms of any accident caused in the form of death or bodily injury, as per the Draft Rules, 2020, it shall be covered by the Insurance procured from a third party. No UA in India can operate without having valid insurance.

10. How does the country plan to manage air traffic?

The Draft UAS Rules establish an Unmanned Aircraft Traffic Management system (UTM) set-up wherein the air traffic would be managed by personnel who has obtained the required training and license to engage in providing air traffic management services. The license for such a position shall be granted by the DGCA. One of the conditions for the grant of such a license is that the personnel are obligated to go through a training course in a certified training organization. Under Schedule X of the Rules, other requirements that the UTM system shall adhere to as a service provider of UAS are also mentioned.

The establishment of the UTM under the rules ensures that the UA traffic is maintained and efficiently integrated with other air traffic.

11. Do you think there could have been more categories for classifying drones introduced in the rules, rather than just weight?

We can also use other categories for the classification of UAS like classifying them on the bases of Size, Range, and endurance as is done by other countries. The technological growth, the devices are becoming compact and lightweight.

12. How does the industry function until the draft rules are finalized?

Until the new rules are streamlined, the CARs on RPAS as issued by DGCA will regulate the industry.

13. Whether the government can overcome the hurdles that previously existed?

The government seems to be determined to overcome the hurdles by enforcing the new regulatory framework.

14. What is controlled and uncontrolled airspace and how are they regulated?

Controlled airspace means an airspace of defined dimensions within which air traffic control service is provided in accordance with the airspace classification. And uncontrolled airspace means airspace where an Air Traffic Control (ATC) service is not necessary or cannot be provided for practical reasons. The director-general of civil aviation specifies the airspace and is then managed by the UAS traffic management service.

15. What is NPNT and how does one comply with it?

NPNT refers to 'No Permission, No Take-Off". It is a software program that enables every RPA (except Nano) to obtain a valid permission through the digital sky platform before operating in India. You can contact your OEM/ Manufacturer for complying with this requirement.

16. What permissions are needed for the usage of Nano drones specifically?

You don't need any permission to fly a Nano drone. However, if you wish to fly in controlled airspace you will need to apply for UIN, UAOP and your UAS shall be NPNT compliant.

17. What are the eligibility requirements for a remote Pilot under the rules?

You should have attained 18 years of age, having passed the 10th exam in English, and undergone training at DGCA approved flying training organization (FTO).

18. What are the permissible areas over which you can fly drones, as this information is not public, and the rules are also silent on the same?

There is an absence of information on permissible areas that act as the biggest roadblock for drone operations. The Rules only state the No

Operational Area under Schedule VIII. Drones cannot be flown in areas specified under Schedule VIII unless they have permission from DGCA. Permission to fly in the controlled airspace can be obtained by filing a flight plan and obtaining a clearance.

19. Whether the model RPAS are the same as the ones flown for recreational activities or as a hobby?

Yes, the Model RPAS are the ones used for recreational activities. The rules are indifferent between the two and the two are similar even in the definitions given in the draft rules, 2020.

20. Will there be new categories of drones like passenger drones or swarm drones in the future as technology develops?

The new UAS Draft rules, 2020 do not mention these categories, but India is moving towards developing these categories with the development of new technologies, so we can expect a later amendment to these rules or CARs by the DGCA that might introduce these types of drones.

21. What are tethered drones? Will they be governed under the same rules?

Tethered drones are the drones that are physically connected through a flexibility link to a power station on the ground. They can be easily retracted and extracted from the winch system they are connected to. The existing CARs and the Draft UAS don't mention these types of drones that could be due to its limited usage in India. For now, it can be assumed that these types of drones should also be compliant with all the certifications, licenses, permits required under the law. If the need arises, the DGCA can develop CARs to govern these types of drones.

22. Should research and development get a separate clause, because of its potential to develop the drone industry?

R&D is an essential function of the drone industry. R&D provision which relaxes the requirement of authorization when a UA is used for R & D purposes should have been included in the rules.

23. Will there be a dedicated unit within the DGCA to specifically govern the drone industry? Do the rules provide for its adoption?

A separate unit under the DGCA should ideally be made to govern the drone industry, this will be extremely beneficial, as the operations of manned and unmanned aircraft can be separated and the efficiency of both the industries can thus be increased. Right now, the rules do not mention a separate unit, but due to the drone industry's growing nature, it can be expected that the operations might become complicated, which can also possibly give rise to a new specialized unit to only specifically deal with drone operations.

24. Can drones be used for surveillance without invasion of privacy?

Drones can be utilized for surveillance whenever need be, but it is possible while it might lead to some invasion of privacy, as the rules also allow for photography. The existing regulatory policy or the Draft Rules, do not deal with the issue of privacy when it comes to the usage of drones, which can give rise to situations of people knowingly or unknowingly invading the privacy of others.

25. Is there a way for providing exemptions in situations like COVID or Locust attack?

The ministry of civil aviation has already provided for conditional exemptions to government entities for COVID-19 related RPAS operations, vide a public notice on 2nd May 2019. This also provides for a separate GARUD portal which will help entities in seeking permission from the central government from carrying out coronavirus related drone operations.

26. Even after getting permission from the concerned authorities under the rules, why is a NOC needed from the Ministry of Defence for data acquisition and mapping operations?

Because data acquisition and mapping operation require the collection of essential data and surveys, that is the reason for stricter implication and a need for NOC from the Ministry of Defence.

27. How can drones help India to fight against COVID?

Help government entities to disinfect, distribute medicines, and essential medical supplies to remote areas and help manage and warn the public against unlawful gathering.

28. Does the government need to build a new policy for drones that caters to the ongoing COVID-19 pandemic and post?

No, as they already have exemption power which even recently has been effective in emergency situations like locust attack, and during the pandemic.

29. What is the law on dropping payloads from the drones? Can it be discharged at all?

As per the new rules, payloads can be carried in the drones, but at the same time they also prohibit releasing any articles from the UAS, while it is in motion. The law needs some clarity as to how it wants to treat the payload and discharging it from the drone.

30. How will the third-party liability with regards to accidents of UAS come into play?

Third Party Insurance: Rule 52 of the Draft rules mandate that no UAS shall operate in India unless there is in existence a valid third-party insurance policy to cover the liability that may arise on account of a mishap involving such UAS causing.

31. Is there a minimum amount of insurance prescribed for UAS operations under the rules?

No minimum account of insurance to be procured is mentioned under the Draft rules however, the IRDA (Insurance Regulatory and Development Authority), and Insurance Regulatory body in India has recently set up a working group to make recommendations on various aspects of insurance coverage for drones. Therefore, after the implementation of the rules, particulars of insurance requirements may be notified in form of a CAR issued by the DGCA.

32. If a UAS is registered in a foreign country but is operating in India, will the rules apply to it?

The rules state that the drones flying in and over India, Draft UAS rules 2020 will be the applicable law.

33. Why did the government choose to enforce rules when CARs were already there for drones?

CARs are less restrictive and have less enforcement power than rules and the penalties are also quite lenient which paves the way to abuse of the law therefore; the rules are needed to provide more stringent and uniform application of laws.

34. What is the procedure for implementing rules after they have been modified and the challenges have been submitted?

- The modified rules will be tabled in the parliament by the end of July 2020. The houses will then sit upon the changes and will decide whether to pass the finalized rules or not.

35. What will happen to CARs 1.0 and 2.0 after the rules come into effect?

- The CARs will cease to exist as soon as the rules are passed by the parliament.

36. What will happen to licenses and permits granted under earlier regulations? Will they have to be renewed or will they survive for the period they were granted?

- The UIN, licenses, and permits will continue to survive under the rules, however, in case of additional requirements, the authorized operator will be required to comply with the same.

37. How long will the government take to bring the UAS rules into effect?

- The government is expected to pass the rules within 2020, considering the urgency and the increased usage of the drones in India.

38. Whether the Annulment of CARs 1.0 and 2.0 will require consultation?

- No, they will not require consultation as CARs would automatically cease to exist and the UAS rules 2020 will substitute them.

39. Can we expect a single-window framework in the final rules?

- No, as there is a larger need to regulate rogue drones and hence the UAS rules are more stringent.

40. Can foreign nationals fly drones in India?

- No, any foreign national cannot fly drones in India. They will have to lease their drones to an Indian organization that will then register and acquire a UIN and UAOP for their drones.

41. What drones can be flown without registering?

- Only Nano drones can be flown without registering within 50 feet above ground level.

42. What are the No-Fly Zones?

- Drones cannot be flown in areas specified as "No Fly Zones", which include areas near airports, international borders, Vijay Chowk in Delhi, State Secretariat Complex in State Capitals, strategic locations, and military installations.

43. Is Drone racing happening in India?

- Yes, the Indian Drone Racing League is India's Official Platform for drone racing, which has been hosting drone races since the year 2016. All the latest updates are also available on their website at https://droneracingindia.com/

44. Can drones be imported as Baggage?

- Yes, it can be, there is no prohibition on the import of drones. However, passengers possessing drones must opt for Red Channel and should declare the same in the separate column in the Customs Declaration Form. The drones are allowed subject to the conditions that the importer should have a license issued by the WPC Wing of the Ministry of Communication and Information Technology for importing the same mentioning proper name, model, and specifications of the goods.

45. Is ETA approval from the WPC wing required for imported drones as well as locally purchased drones?

- ETA approval from the WPC wing of the Department of Communications is required for all equipment working in India in de-licensed frequency bands. Therefore, for both imported drones as well as a locally purchased drone, this approval is required.

46. Do general product liability rules apply to the manufacturer of Drones?

- CAR 1.0 and UAS Draft Rules do not specifically deal with or mention product liability. However, in India, other regulations deal with the liability for manufactured goods that can turn out to be defective or technically faulty. These regulations include the Consumers Protection Act, 2019, and general principles of Tort law.

47. How does one determine the fees to be paid for different licenses, registrations, and permits obtained under the UAS Draft Rules, 2020?

- Schedule XI of the Draft rules mentions the details of the fees payable for each process.

48. What is the difference between a Drone and an Unmanned Aircraft?

- There is no difference between the two. The drone is terminology for Unmanned Aircraft.

49. Do drones need to be registered?

- Yes, drones are requires to be registered . There is no exemption given by government when it comes to registration.

50. How to register a drone?

- Registration can be done by obtaining a Unique Identification Number (UIN) under the rules. Application is made to the DGCA in the manner and procedure prescribed in Schedule III of the Draft rules for obtaining a UIN for your unmanned aircraft.

51. What is the use of UIN?

- UIN is the unique identification number that authorized specifically to a particular drone by the DGCA. Once you obtain the UIN, it shall be affixed on the UA in an identifiable and visible manner.

52. What is the penalty for non-compliance with the draft rules?

- If a person contravenes or fails to comply with any provision of the rules, the penalty for it is laid down in Schedule XII.

53. What are the Qualifications required by a remote Pilot for flying a UAS?

- The remote pilot flying a drone needs to be of 18 years of age. Apart from that, they should also undergo a specialized ground and practical training in the DGCA authorized Flight Training Organisations. (FTOs). Annexure IX of the CAR mentions the curriculum to be followed by these FTOs while imparting the training. However, the pilots flying a Nano or Micro category drone are exempted from such training under CARs.

54. Can the Nano and Microdrones be flown by anyone without obtaining any training/ approval from the DGCA?

- Yes, as per current law, the person flying a Nano, or a Micro drone does not need any mandatory qualifications, training or licenses.

55. To resell the UAS to another person, what procedure is to be followed?

- Before the transfer of the UAS, the seller shall notify the DGCA of its change in ownership. The UIN number of the UA then must be deregistered and the buyer has to apply for a fresh UIN.

56. What all exemptions are given to the Nano Category drones under the law?

- The nano category drones are given the following exemptions:
- No import clearance is required under the CAR
- No requirement for acquiring a Unique Identification Number (UIN), if flying up to 50 feet
- No need for acquiring an operator permit if flying within 50 feet altitude

- No need to inform the DGCA about an accident involving the drone
- The pilots flying nano drones are not required to undergo training
- No need to adhere to the equipment requirements under para 11 of the CAR
- No need to obtain permission before each flight if operating below 50 feet.
- No need to provide DGCA with a Certificate of Compliance along with NPNT compliance.

57. Whether the operators or the owners of UA required to maintain a maintenance log of their UA?

- Rule 16 of the Draft Rules states that it shall be mandatory for every importer or manufacturer in India to supply a maintenance manual to authorized traders, owners, or operators. This manual shall contain the requirements and procedures of maintenance of the UAS.
- The rule also mandates every owner and operator to ensure that their UA is maintained as per the manual. They are also required to maintain a record of such maintenance.

58. Can drones be flown beyond visual line of sight?

- As per the current law, drones are only allowed to be flown within the visual line of sight of the pilot and the observer.

59. What is the procedure if an operator wants to fly their UAVs over the no-fly zone?

- Flying UAV over the no-fly zone is prohibited. However, DGCA may authorize Government authorities or any other airport operator on a case-to-case basis only under exceptional circumstances.

60. How are autonomous UAVs operated?

- An "autonomous drone" is piloted by software instead of a human, an autonomous drone is part of a UAS by definition, as it requires a complete system to operate.

61. Where are the filling instructions for UIN/UAOP?

- The instructions for filling all applications are present in the Digital Sky Manual. The Manual will be available on the DGCA website homepage www.dgca.nic.in and also in the Digital Sky Portal homepage.

62. How to mark a UIN on Unmanned Aircraft?

- After obtaining a UIN, one can engrave it on a fire-resistant plate and firmly affix it on your unmanned aircraft. The number is to be affixed in all circumstances even during routine handling, flight operations, etc.

63. Is it allowed to fly UAS inside the building without having a UIN?

- There is no UIN requirement for Nano. However, for any drone other than a NANO drone, they must register.

64. What is the procedure for reselling an Unmanned Aircraft?

- Unmanned aircraft if issued with UIN, cannot be transferred or disposed of without permission from DGCA. There is a requirement for cancellation of UIN and the buyer will have to apply for fresh UIN through Digital Sky Platform.

VIII. <u>CHAPTER 10</u>

<u>Bibliography</u>

1.	https://www.mondaq.com/india/aviation/885694/drone-law-policy-developments-in-india-welcoming-drones-in-2020
2.	https://www.lexology.com/library/detail.aspx?g=3270f8b8-c172-4f01-bfd6-9a2518f92775
3.	https://www.drishtiias.com/daily-updates/daily-news-analysis/national-anti-drone-guidelines
4.	https://www.civilaviation.gov.in/sites/default/files/MoCA_Public%20Notice_Issuance_of_DAN_08_June_2020.pdf
5.	https://www.civilaviation.gov.in/sites/default/files/Counter_rogue_drone_guidelnes_NSCS.pdf
6.	https://dgca.gov.in/digigov-portal/?dynamicPage=dynamicPdf/130574958&maincivilAviationRequirements/6/0/viewDynamicRulesReq
7.	https://dgca.gov.in/digigov-portal/jsp/dgca/homePage/viewPDF.jsp?page=InventoryList/headerblock/drones/FTC1_2019.pdf
8.	https://dgca.gov.in/digigov-portal/jsp/dgca/homePage/viewPDF.jsp?page=InventoryList/headerblock/drones/DGCA%20RPAS%20Guidance%20Manual.pdf
9.	https://www.anratechnologies.com/home/tag/better-drones/
10.	https://www.drishtiias.com/daily-updates/daily-news-analysis/draft-unmanned-aircraft-system-uas-rules-2020
11.	https://www.livelaw.in/columns/unboxing-the-proposed-drone-laws-an-analysis-of-the-new-draft-rules-on-uasdrones-in-india-158487?infinitescroll=1
12.	https://www.mydronelab.com/blog/commercial-use-of-drones.html
13.	https://www.businessinsider.in/tech/news/drone-technology-uses-and-applications-for-commercial-industrial-and-military-drones-in-2020-and-the-future/articleshow/72874958.cms
14.	https://yourstory.com/2019/06/india-flying-drone-technology
15.	https://www.businesstoday.in/magazine/the-buzz/is-it-time-for-drone-taxis/story/304037.html#:~:text=India%20is%20also%20exploring%20the,drone%20taxi%20service%20in%20Mumbai.
16.	https://www.constructionweekonline.in/business/13323-ministry-of-civil-aviation-grants-approval-to-13-consortia-to-operate-drones
17.	https://dronelife.com/2020/06/08/drones-in-india-bvlos-drone-delivery/

18. https://economictimes.indiatimes.com/blogs/et-commentary/covid-19-responses-show-need-to-revisit-indias-drone-policy/
19. https://www.orfonline.org/expert-speak/flight-opportunity-covid19-india-drone-industry-68059/
20. http://www.businessworld.in/article/India-s-Rural-Poor-May-Lose-Out-As-Drones-Map-Village-Land/27-04-2020-190351/
21. https://www.ikigailaw.com/a-comparison-of-the-draft-unmanned-aircraft-system-rules-2020-and-the-civil-aviation-requirements-on-remotely-piloted-aircraft-system-2018/
22. https://www.civilaviation.gov.in/sites/default/files/Public%20notice_GARUD_Exemptions%20for%20Covid-19_2%20May%202020.pdf
23. https://garud.civilaviation.gov.in/public_info
24. https://www.expresscomputer.in/indiaincfightscovid19/covid-19-garud-portal-launched-to-grant-exemption-for-drone-rpa-usage/54879/
25. https://en.wikipedia.org/wiki/List_of_unmanned_aerial_vehicles
26. https://www.orfonline.org/research/drones-guidelines-regulations-and-policy-gaps-in-india/
27. https://www.pwc.in/consulting/financial-services/fintech/fintech-insights/data-on-wings-a-close-look-at-drones-in-india.html
28. http://www.nishithdesai.com/fileadmin/user_upload/pdfs/Research_Papers/India-Opens-Skies-for-Drones-Legal-Tax-Analysis.pdf

29. https://inc42.com/features/the-sorry-state-of-drones-in-india-startups-stuck-in-license-raj-amid-rising-cost-of-innovation/
30. https://inc42.com/features/how-the-governments-half-baked-drone-policy-has-grounded-startups-in-india/
31. https://factordaily.com/drone-woes-as-regulatory-delays-persist-companies-seek-provisional-fixes-to-fly-drones-in-india/
32. https://www.civilaviation.gov.in/sites/default/files/MoCA_Order_Conditional_Exemption_for_anti_locust_operations_21_May_2020.pdf
33. http://dronefederation.in/2020/05/21/ministry-of-civil-aviation-grants-exemptions-to-ministry-of-agriculture-for-utilising-drones-for-spraying-pesticides-on-crops-for-anti-locust-operations/
34. https://tech.economictimes.indiatimes.com/news/technology/india-likely-to-use-drones-to-beat-back-locusts/75901945
35. https://www.civilaviation.gov.in/sites/default/files/Public%20notice_GARUD_Exemptions%20for%20Covid-19_2%20May%202020.pdf
36. https://www.expresscomputer.in/indiaincfightscovid19/covid-19-garud-portal-launched-to-grant-exemption-for-drone-rpa-usage/54879/

37. https://www.forbes.com/sites/anuraghunathan/2020/06/19/how-drones-are-helping-india-fight-the-coronavirus-pandemic/#4507292f3768

38. https://www.business-standard.com/article/technology/sanitation-aerial-alerts-make-drones-new-soldiers-in-war-against-covid-19-120041601525_1.html

39. https://www.medianama.com/2020/04/223-drones-to-map-rural-india/

40. https://www.medianama.com/2020/06/223-digital-mapping-villages-india/

41. https://medium.com/indshine/drones-are-helping-indian-railways-to-wrap-fast-track-projects-ahead-2019-elections-e572540ffbae

42. https://www.investindia.gov.in/team-india-blogs/growing-market-drone-technologies-india

43. https://energy.economictimes.indiatimes.com/news/oil-and-gas/gail-hires-drones-to-secure-gas-pipelines/61948751

44. https://www.expresscomputer.in/news/the-state-of-drone-market-in-india/44529/#:~:text=According%20to%20a%20report%20by,18%25%20during%202017%2D23.

45. https://www.livemint.com/Politics/ZDib5YWR1G2Mcuth1kbwyO/Drones-scan-floodhit-Uttarakhand.html

46. [http://www.fao.org/3/I8494EN/i8494en.pdf

47. https://factordaily.com/drones-for-precision-agriculture-in-india/

48. https://www.investindia.gov.in/team-india-blogs/growing-market-drone-technologies-india

49. https://www.defenseworld.net/news/25688/India_to_Develop_Air_launched_Swarm_Drone_Systems__Stealthy_AI_enabled_Combat_Drones#.XwdNOygzY2x

50. https://theprint.in/defence/hal-ties-up-with-israeli-firm-dynamatic-technologies-to-manufacture-drones/360252/

51. https://economictimes.indiatimes.com/news/defence/indigenous-device-all-set-to-track-and-kill-enemy-drones/articleshow/64493188.cms?from=mdr

52. https://www.tataadvancedsystems.com/static.php?id

53. https://www.dynamatics.com/security.shtm

54. https://www.lnt-defence.com/our-offerings/missiles-aerospace/unmanned-aerial-systems-targe

55. https://garudauav.com/

56. https://internetdemocracy.in/reports/submission-in-response-to-the-draft-unmanned-aircraft-drone-rules-2020/

57. https://www.medianama.com/2020/07/223-digisky-platform-live/

58. http://www.businessworld.in/article/India-s-first-NPNT-compliant-drone-flight-successfully-completed/03-07-2020-293785/

59. https://www.mondaq.com/india/aviation/885694/drone-law-policy-developments-in-india-welcoming-drones-in-2020

60. https://www.cbic.gov.in/resources//htdocs-cbec/customs/cs-circulars/cs-circulars-2019/Circular-No-32-2019.pdf;jsessionid=989EF64D6E9B19DB263D10141A9464D2

61. https://geoawesomeness.com/flying-drones-in-india/-

62. https://learndrone.tech/can-i-import-a-drone-to-india/

63. http://www.ficci.in/Sedocument/20506/FICCI-Recommendations-on-the-Draft-UAS-Rules-2020.pdf

64. https://www.medianama.com/2020/07/223-digisky-platform-live/

65. http://www.businessworld.in/article/India-s-first-NPNT-compliant-drone-flight-successfully-completed/03-07-2020-293785/

66. https://www.civilaviation.gov.in/sites/default/files/Presentation_on_Drones.pdf

67. https://siteofthedrones.com/types-of-drones/

68. https://www.auav.com.au/articles/drone-types/

69. https://www.medianama.com/2020/06/223-drone-pilot-training-schools-india/

70. https://www.medianama.com/wp-content/uploads/FTC02_2020Draft_June2020-1.pdf   -   Flying Training Circular 2 of 2020 (DGCA)

71. https://www.thehindu.com/news/cities/mumbai/more-drone-pilot-training-schools-in-offing/article31855565.ece

72. https://www.indianinstituteofdrones.com/

73. https://www.global-aero.com/unmanned-aircraft-systems-uas-insurance/

74. https://www.livelaw.in/columns/unboxing-the-proposed-drone-laws-an-analysis-of-the-new-draft-rules-on-uasdrones-in-india-158487

75. https://medium.com/frontier-technology-livestreaming/drone-regulations-in-india-simplified-f5740d088670

76. https://www.thehindubusinessline.com/economy/irdai-sets-up-panel-on-insurance-for-use-drones/article31915752.ece-

77. https://drone-traveller.com/drone-insurance/

78. https://www.nsinsurance.com/news/hdfc-ergo-drone-insurance-india/#:~:text=India%2Dbased%20insurer%20HDFC%20ERGO,property%20damage%20and%20bodily%20injuries.

79. https://taxguru.in/corporate-law/drone-technology-regulations.html

80. https://percepto.co/what-are-the-differences-between-uav-uas-and-autonomous-drones/

81. https://www.ikigailaw.com/a-comparison-of-the-draft-unmanned-aircraft-system-rules-2020-and-the-civil-aviation-requirements-on-remotely-piloted-aircraft-system-2018/#_ftn4

82. https://qz.com/india/1543681/indias-new-drone-policy-is-shortsighted-heres-why/
83. https://filmora.wondershare.com/drones/top-heavy-lift-drones.html
84. http://www.legalserviceindia.com/legal/article-676-legal-analysis-of-right-to-privacy-in-india.html
85. http://grinddrone.com/drone-features/drone-components
86. https://www.gpsworld.com/altitude-angel-powers-bvlos-flights-in-india-with-sagar-defence/
87. https://dronelife.com/2020/06/08/drones-in-india-bvlos-drone-delivery/#:~:text=Drones%20in%20India%3A%20BVLOS%20Drone%20Delivery%20for%20Food%20and%20Medicine,-Posted%20By%3A%20Miriam&text=Just%20a%20year%20after%20India,exemptions%20to%20operate%20drones%20BVLOS.
88. https://indianacademyofdrones.com/beyond-visual-line-of-sight/#:~:text=The%20Telangana%20government%20has%20shown,medical%20drone%20delivery%20company%20Zipline.
89. https://www.geospatialworld.net/news/indian-government-announces-drone-policy-2-0/
90. https://www.commercialuavnews.com/infrastructure/india-opens-the-sky-for-drones-under-no-permission-no-takeoff-npnt-system
91. https://www.geospatialworld.net/blogs/how-drones-are-being-used-to-combat-covid-19/
92. https://timesofindia.indiatimes.com/videos/city/mumbai/covid-19-outbreak-mumbai-police-using-drones-to-monitor-situation-amid-curfew/videoshow/74820827.cms

93. http://www.xinhuanet.com/english/2020-08/02/c_139259400.htm
94. https://www.ndtv.com/india-news/covid-19-heres-how-drones-helping-india-in-fight-against-coronavirus-2211888
95. https://timesofindia.indiatimes.com/india/locust-menace-fao-asks-india-to-be-on-high-alert-for-next-4-weeks/articleshow/76798768.cms
96. https://www.bbc.com/news/world-asia-india-52804981#:~:text=Locust%20swarms%20destroy%20crops%20across%20India&text=Large%20and%20aggressive%20swarms%20of,are%20the%20worst%20affected%20states.
97. https://pib.gov.in/newsite/PrintRelease.aspx?relid=210035
98. https://www.thehindu.com/news/national/other-states/locust-attack-about-90000-hectares-hit-in-20-rajasthan-districts/article31694494.ece#:~:text=The%20Union%20Ministry%20of%20Civil,20%20districts%20of%20the%20State.
99. https://tech.economictimes.indiatimes.com/news/technology/dgca-allows-use-of-drones-at-night-to-ward-off-locusts/76692662

100. https://www.pwc.in/assets/pdfs/research-insights/2020/preparing-for-takeoff.pdf
101. https://www.altiuas.com/drone-surveillance/
102. https://www.zdnet.com/article/best-security-surveillance-drones-for-business/
103. https://www.airbornedrones.co/surveillance-and-security/
104. https://timesofindia.indiatimes.com/business/india-business/aviation-ministry-allows-indianoil-to-use-drones-for-aerial-surveillance-of-delhi-panipat-pipeline/articleshow/76861665.cms
105. https://www.concreteshowindia.com/blog/drones-in-indian-construction-industry/
106. https://wii.gov.in/images/images/documents/publications/rr_2019_uv.pdf
107. https://medium.com/indshine/nhai-is-set-to-map-a-large-part-of-the-indian-road-network-using-drones-11b28bcf0ee1
108. https://www.ideaforge.co.in/blog/drones-disaster-relief/
109. https://www.bgr.in/features/karnataka-floods-2018-exclusive-look-drone-technology-helped-rescue-efforts-coorg-kodagu-august-netra-drones-ankit-mehta-686383/
110. https://www.aerialphoto.in/
111. https://wingtra.com/drone-mapping-applications/surveying-gis/#:~:text=Land%20surveying%20%2F%20cartography,or%20difficult%20to%20access%20environments.
112. https://blog.dronetrader.com/top-passenger-drones-helicopters-drone-taxis/
113. https://www.dronezon.com/drones-for-good/drone-parcel-pizza-delivery-service/
114. https://uavcoach.com/types-of-drones/#1
115. https://www.dronethusiast.com/best-professional-drones/
116. https://mydeardrone.com/uses/
117. https://www.cbinsights.com/research/drone-impact-society-uav/#:~:text=Disease%20Control,-Tracking%20animals%20also&text=In%20a%20similar%20vein%2C%20Microsoft,prevent%20epidemics%20before%20they%20begin.
118. https://www.dronezon.com/drones-for-good/wildlife-conservation-protection-using-anti-poaching-drones-technology/
119. https://insideunmannedsystems.com/drones-transform-archaeology/
120. https://economictimes.indiatimes.com/news/politics-and-nation/weather-forecasting-in-times-of-extreme-weather-events/articleshow/69805112.cms
121. https://www.civilaviation.gov.in/sites/default/files/MoCA%20Order_6%20green%20zones_03%20April%202020.pdf

122. https://www.manifestias.com/2020/05/01/drone-regulation/#:~:text=Yellow%20signifies%20airspace%20requiring%20Air,Sky%20Platform%20to%20commence%20operations.
123. https://www.civilaviation.gov.in/sites/default/files/Presentation_on_Drones.pdf
124. https://public-prd-dgca.s3.ap-south-
125. 1.amazonaws.com/InventoryList/headerblock/drones/D3X-X1.pdf
126. https://www.mdpi.com/2504-446X/3/1/10/htm
127. https://www.ecotourism.org.au/news/how-drones-help-conservation-efforts/
128. https://www.ee.co.za/article/the-use-of-drones-in-conservation.html
129. https://www.drdrone.ca/blogs/drone-news-drone-help-blog/howdronesarerevolutionizingtheenergyindustry
130. https://www.drdrone.ca/blogs/drone-news-drone-help-blog/drones-in-energy-industry
131. http://www.doctorpreneurs.com/9-drones-that-will-revolutionise-healthcare/
132. https://www.dronesinhealthcare.com/
133. https://www.psqh.com/analysis/drones-could-be-the-future-of-healthcare/
134. https://www.epiphan.com/blog/4-ways-to-use-live-stream-drone-footage/
135. https://uavcoach.com/professional-drones/
136. https://wingtra.com/drone-mapping-applications/mining-and-aggregates/#:~:text=Drone%20aerial%20images%20can%20be,can%20now%20be%20performed%20easily.
137. https://www.airoboticsdrones.com/mining/
138. https://www.nsenergybusiness.com/features/drones-in-mining-trends/
139. https://www.pixpa.com/blog/aerial-photography-using-drones
140. https://digicamhelp.com/how-to/special-subjects/6-reasons-photographers-use-drones/
141. https://www.digitalcameraworld.com/buying-guides/the-10-best-camera-drones
142. https://www.microdrones.com/en/industry-experts/science-and-academic-research/
143. https://thetius.com/how-are-aerial-drones-being-used-in-maritime/
144. https://www.commercialuavnews.com/security/4-ways-drones-maritime-offshore-services
145. https://www.ncbi.nlm.nih.gov/pmc/articles/PMC7206421/
146. https://www.futurefarming.com/Machinery/Articles/2019/4/India n-state-turns-to-drones-to-modernise-agriculture-

413234E/#:~:text=Drones%20can%20help%20farmers%20calculat
e,the%20prices%20of%20agriculture%20drones.

147. https://startuptalky.com/agriculture-startups-in-india/
148. https://uwmadscience.news.wisc.edu/atmospheric-
science/forecast-uncertain-an-unmanned-drone-will-fly-into-
hurricane-matthew/
149. https://www.dronepilotgroundschool.com/visual-observer/
150. https://www.nishithdesai.com/information/news-storage/news-
details/article/future-of-drones-in-india-draft-rules-2020.html
151. https://ethz.ch/content/dam/ethz/special-interest/mtec/pom-
dam/documents/Drones%20in%20warehouse%20opeations_PO
M%20whitepaper%202019_Final.pdf
152. Globalaviationsummit.in/documents/VISION-2040-FOR-THE-CIVIL-
AVIATION-INDUSTRY-IN-INDIA.pdf
153. Civilaviation.gov.in/sites/default/files/Presentation_on_Drones.pd
f
154. Goatek.com/drone-applications-in-waste-management/
155. Flyguys.com/uav-industries/hospitality-photography/
156. Microdrones.com/en/industry-experts/inspection/
157. Space.com/nasa-drone-exploration-dragonfly-mars-
helicopter.html
158. Brookings.edu/blog/techtank/2018/12/14how-emergency-
responders-are-using-drones-to-save-lives
159. liss.nic.in/eMagazine/v2i1/5.pdf
160. Elearningindustry.com/drones-in-the-classroom-5ways-
cherishing-students-passion-technology
161. Transitive.com/knowledgebase/how-does-a-uav-navigation-
system-work/
162. http://www.ipface.org/pdfs/Brochure_SIPEIT.pdf
163. https://www.standupmitra.in/
164. http://www.serb.gov.in/home.php
165. https://www.mudra.org.in/

166. https://sidbi.in/en
167. https://www.nsic.co.in/Schemes/Raw-Material-Against-BG.aspx
168. https://www.nsic.co.in/Schemes/Credit-Facilitation-Through-
Bank.aspx
169. https://msme.gov.in/marketing-promotion-schemes
170. https://www.cgtmse.in/files/CGS-I.pdf
171. https://www.startupindia.gov.in/content/dam/invest-
india/Templates/public/Central%20Sector%20Schemes%20for%2
0MSMEs.pdf
172. https://www.india.gov.in/spotlight/building-atmanirbhar-bharat-
overcoming-covid-19
173. https://corporatefinanceinstitute.com/resources/knowledge/val
uation/startup-valuation-

methods/#:~:text=The%20market%20multiple%20method%20works,using%20the%20base%20market%20multiple.

174. https://www.thequint.com/tech-and-auto/after-drone-legalisation-startups-expect-fundings
175. https://smejoinup.com/differences-between-private-limited-and-llp-company/
176. https://static.investindia.gov.in/s3fs-public/2019-06/Business%20Guide%20v13_Non-Paginated_English.pdf
177. https://static.investindia.gov.in/s3fs-public/2020-07/doing-business-in-india-2020_0.pdf
178. https://www.mondaq.com/india/aviation/971556/drone-laws
179. https://www.droneii.com/money-talks-2019-drone-investments-break-new-records
180. https://www.droneii.com/project/drone-market-report-2020-2025

9 798688 382617